MISSION ACCOMPLISHED

Mission Accomplished

P. A. RICKSON
and
A. HOLLIDAY

BOOK CLUB EDITION

This edition published by
Purnell Book Services, Limited,
St. Giles House, 49/50 Poland Street, W1A 2LG,
by arrangement with
WILLIAM KIMBER & CO. LIMITED

Typset by
Specialised Offset Services Ltd. Liverpool
and printed and bound in Great Britain by
Robert MacLehose & Co. Ltd, Glasgow

CONTENTS

Page

LIST OF ILLUSTRATIONS

Operation 'Upkeep'

Operation Jericho

Operation Thunderbolt

PREFACE

Of the many daring allied and enemy air operations carried out in World War II, a number, because of the particular circumstances involved, could be said to be 'one off' type missions.

Some, despite their meticulous planning and courageous execution, were doomed to failure from the start and achieved little or nothing. Others however, had sufficient ingenuity and audacity built into them during their conception to ensure a considerable amount of success. The stories of three missions, two British and one German, which were outstandingly successful in achieving their specific aims are related in this book.

Operation 'Upkeep' — the dams raid — revolved around the precise delivery of a new weapon, the 'bouncing' bomb. This operation called for the most accurate of low level precision bombing, and became a landmark in this particular technique: operation 'Jericho' was another low level mission in which the RAF achieved results as dramatic as the toppling of the walls of Jericho in the biblical story, and which later became the forerunner of many similar operations: operation 'Thunderbolt', although basically a German Naval operation could never have been attempted without the full co-operation of the German Air Force. The defensive air-support needed to ensure the success of this mission has not been fully told before.

Practically all mission were, in the final analysis, a gamble. With so many outside and unknown factors involved, a relatively small detail could spell the difference between success or failure of an operation. In these three particular cases — the gamble paid off.

P. Rickson
A. Holliday

Kingston upon Thames
June 1974

TO
. . . . 'The long,
and the short,
and the tall' . . . .

OPERATION UPKEEP

Premonition

In a little town in the Ruhr, Oberburgermeister Dillgardt was worried. He was afraid that one day, he didn't know when, some enemy bombers would come and try to bomb the dams. These dams, hidden in the great Ruhr Mountains, acted as huge reservoirs to the complex underground water system that supplied the Ruhr with water for both industrial and domestic use.

With his knowledge of the vast underground water system, Dillgardt knew that an enemy only needed to knock out two of the dams — the Moehne and the Sorpe — to bring German heavy industry in the Ruhr to a grinding halt. So it was with these thoughts in mind that he went seeking the advice of experts. Telling them his fears, he was surprised at their answers. They assured him that the walls of the dams would withstand any bombing attack an enemy could throw at them. They said there was no known bomb effective enough to destroy the dams.

In spite of these reassurances, Dillgardt was not satisfied. He went and inspected for himself the defences around the dams, and all he could find were some anti-torpedo nets floating in the water, held away from the dam face by booms. Admittedly there were one or two anti-aircraft guns, but in Dillgardt's opinion the defences of the dams left a lot to be desired.

He still wasn't satisfied that the experts were correct in their assumptions, however, and when he bought a book called *The Curse of Bombing* by Camille Rougeron, he found in it a chapter dealing with the bombing of dams. Rougeron described the most practical way to bomb a dam, stating that if the bomb was dropped in the water near the face of the dam, the compressive effect of the water would direct the full effect of the bomb's blast at the dam's wall.

This was just what Dillgardt feared. It confirmed his fears that experts could be wrong. The next step as far as he could see was to write to the military authorities. This he did, in a long letter to the Chiefs of Staff of the Wehrmacht at their Headquarters in Meunster. He gave them all the details of the potential damage to industry, of the widespread flooding and so on, and he pleaded with them to strengthen their defences on the dams.

A few days later, he received a reply from the Wehrmacht. It was polite, thanking him for his letter and the interest he had shown for the safety of the Dams; the matter, he was assured, would be looked into. That was all it said, and there is no doubt that the Chiefs of Staff thought that would be the end of it. They had already put Dillgardt down as some sort of crank. His letter was carefully filed away with due thoroughness, together with a copy of their reply.

The date at this point was 29th August, 1939 — before war between Germany and Britain had even begun! During the next three years, however, the file held at Muenster containing Dillgardt's letter was to grow quite thick. It was closed when the Chiefs of Staff increased the number of anti-aircraft guns around the Dams and wrote a final letter to Dillgardt telling him that there was no longer any need for him to advise them.

Oberburgermeister Dillgardt was a very unusual man, for he, as a civilian, had foreseen the importance of the Dams. In his constant letters to the Wehrmacht, he had told them not only what was going to happen, but the actual month of the year in which it would happen. For he knew the Dams to be at their fullest in May, so he had warned the Chiefs of Staff, well in advance, of something that was to come true on the night of 16th-17th May, 1943, four years after he had first foreseen the danger!

Prelude

Although Oberburgermeister Dillgardt had been worried about the measures to safeguard the Dams from an aerial attack, the experts had been equally correct when they told him that there was at the time no bomb capable of damaging the Dams. This was the problem facing another man, who like Dillgardt, was concerned about the Ruhr Dams. His problem was to make Dillgardt's fears come true, for he was to design the bomb that would make history.

The name of the man was Barnes Wallis, and he was working for an aircraft company, Vickers Armstrong Ltd., at Weybridge, in

Barnes Wallis

England. He was a happily married man, with children, who loved nothing more than to be with his family. His main dread was war, which is strange in a man who had spent his life in a design office dedicated to building bomber aircraft, and other warlike things. But Wallis, as with the other people doing similar jobs, considered that if there was going to be a war, then his country should be well enough equipped to give any aggressor as good, if not better than he gave. It was to be hoped that things would never come to that, for Wallis wanted nothing more out of life than to live a happy, peaceful one.

He enjoyed camping, sailing, gardening and all the other family activities. To see him one would never believe he was to become famous, for he did not strike one as anyone out of the ordinary at first sight. But this would be wrong, for that tall grey-haired man with the soft grey smiling eyes and the mild manners was one of Britain's top designers. His efforts were to play a big part in making Germany wish she had never started a war, for he was to design the bomb that would blast great holes in the Ruhr Dams. Not only that, but he was to be instrumental in the forming of a unique bomber squadron to do this job, trained solely, at first, for this one raid, but carrying on to do work of a similar specialist nature. The same squadron is operational today, and the men in it have the same high ideals its founders built up.

The day Britain went to war with Germany found Wallis back in his office at Weybridge again. He had been taking a few days camping holiday in Dorset with his family, and when he heard that hostilities had broken out was anxious to get back to work. He asked his wife and family to remain in Dorset for the time being, until things sorted themselves out a little more.

Time passed slowly in the early days of the war in Britain. There was no *Blitzkrieg* as there had been in other European countries. Things seemed to carry on as normal in a stage known as the 'Phoney War'. It was during this time that Wallis turned his attention to finding a way to shorten the war. Although it had only just started with Britain, it had been going on in Europe for several months. What is more, the Germans had been winning all the battles.

Pondering over the question of how to shorten the war, Wallis drew up a list of possible key targets for bombing. These consisted of such things as coal mines, oil wells and hydro-electric power, or dams. It is logical to suppose that if you cut one of these three vital items from an enemy's supply, then he cannot produce his armaments, or mobilize his armies. If you could deprive him of all three, he can no longer wage war. That was Wallis's line of reasoning, and it was to prove correct in World War II.

Taking each item individually, Wallis weighed up the best method of destruction, with the armaments at the disposal of Britain at the time. He came to this conclusion:-

1. Coal mines could not be bombed successfully.
2. Oil wells could be bombed, but at this stage of the war the RAF had no aircraft capable of the range. Germany's main source of oil was in far off Rumania. Out of range of British based bombers.
3. The Ruhr Dams could be bombed, but the RAF had no bomb powerful enough to destroy them.

It was the last item, then, that Wallis chose to look into. No one realised in those early days of the war to what extent bombs would develop. One man did realise the sad state of stagnation into which Britain's ordnance had sunk, after so many years of peaceful existence. The bombs that were being used by the RAF were mostly of First World War vintage, and the maximum weight of the largest of them was 500-lbs. Wallis worked out that he would require a bomb of 10 tons, with 7 tons of explosive! There was no such bomb in existence, and even if there had been, there was no aircraft designed that could carry it.

But so far Wallis had no detailed information on the bombing of dams, unlike meister Dillgardt. Had Wallis read Rougeron's book he would no doubt have solved his problem sooner. He was working on the right lines, but finding the correct solution was to take time. Meanwhile, much of his time was taken up in calculations which were used, not in the design of the Dam-busting bomb, but for the later 'Grand Slam'. Wallis had the idea that if you dropped *one* heavy bomb from a high flying aircraft, the weight of the bomb, plus its speed of fall, would bury it deep in the earth. The resultant explosion would send out great shock waves rather like those of an earthquake, which would crumble the foundations of a wall such as that of a dam.

From his calculations Wallis was convinced this was the way to set about the destruction of the Dams. The next problem was to design the bomb, and an aircraft to carry it. So it was a case of 'back to the drawing board'. Eventually a design emerged, which he called his 'Victory Bomber'. But dreaming up a war-winning idea is one thing. Selling the idea to the people that count is another.

Just at this particular time in the war, British troops were straggling home from the beaches of Dunkirk, and the nation was beginning to realise how ill equipped it was for war. An ideal time for Wallis to try and sell his idea of a 'Victory Bomber'. Even so, how to go about it? Wallis did what he'd done many times before. He prepared a paper, the subject of which he called the 'Earthquake Bomb'. This paper was then sent to the various departments interested in Whitehall, ending up on various official desks, as had many of his previous papers. He was well used to the proper procedure for putting ideas forward.

Two questions face the Government Departments concerned with the manufacture of new weapons. Will they work? Are they worth the expense? The money to pay for all military purchases comes out of the taxpayers' pocket, so each idea that is put forward is given careful scrutiny. Many cranky ideas come before the authorities especially in war time. Some ideas are winners, some are doubtful, but the majority are outright losers. If the committee think they have a winner, they send it to the Service conerned, who again look at it. They weigh it up, assess it's prospects and return a verdict to the original committee.

This paper of Wallis's on the 'Earthquake Bomb' did arouse a certain amount of interest, but it had its faults. The main flaw was the aircraft required to carry such a bomb. Most people thought that the idea was sound, but that the bomb was not a good proposition without the aeroplane. Just at that time, every factory worker was busy on other projects equally important, and in this instance Wallis was asking to stop completely the production of one factory for a while. It was doubtful if a bomber could be found to carry the bomb, even if the latter was built — and the length of time required to develop a new aircraft can amount to years.

And so Wallis was doomed to disappointment. His project was turned down. This did not stop him, however, for he spent the next few months writing a paper of a simpler nature, so easy to understand that any layman would have no difficulty in understanding it. The paper was entitled 'A Note on a Method of Destroying the Axis Powers'. This 'note' was quite a thick volume. Seventy copies of it were printed and Wallis distributed them to all leading scientists, politicians and Service chiefs; then he sat back to await results. He did not have to wait long. One of the first to call was a man from M.I.5. He was most upset that Wallis should have sent out *Classified* information in such a way; he was to get palpitations a few seconds later when Wallis mildy told him that he had distributed seventy copies!

Other results of a positive nature did come shortly after, however. A Group Captain Winterbottom had received a copy and was so interested that he showed it to Sir Henry Tizard, who was scientific adviser to the Ministry of Aircraft Production. On his recommendation a committee was set up to study Wallis's proposals carefully. One committee led to the formation of another committee, but it was something. The suggestion of the second committee was that experiments should be carried out on a model of one of the dams. This was done, but the results showed that a ten-ton bomb would not achieve the required results. Wallis's calculations were not correct. Disappointed, the experiment was allowed to go on until a hole was blown in the wall of the model. After fresh calculations were done it was found that a *thirty*-ton bomb would be needed!

Although bitterly disappointed, Wallis refused to give up. It was this grim determination that set him on the right track. True, the results of his experiments had proved his calculations wrong, but they also showed him the need to start afresh. So far he had relied on dropping a bomb in the waters of the dam, fifty feet away from the wall of the dam itself. He had been relying on the shock waves to crumble the dam wall from this distance. In fact even Rougeron had been wrong on this point in his book. But the basic thinking was still correct, so Wallis decided to try further experiments. He knew that if a bomb was exploded *against* the face of the dam wall, under water, the bomb required would be smaller. Now how could one place such a bomb in that position?

The idea came slowly, from a memory of his children at play in the sea the year before, throwing pebbles so that they skipped along the top of the water. But would it work? If it did a completely new type of bomb would have to be devised. He started experiments in his own back garden, using an old bath tub full of water and aiming golf balls at it from a catapault type platform a few feet away. The experiment was a complete success. When the committee next met, Wallis was more confident. Although the results of the first set of experiments had proved negative, he asked permission for a further set, stating he had a new idea for delivery of the bomb. He was granted permission.

Two new inventions were now in production that were to come to Wallis's aid. The first was a new explosive called R.D.X. The second was a new bomber called the Lancaster. He used both of them in the new set of experiments and from the results concluded that he would be able to blow a hole clean through the Moehne Dam with a 5-ton bomb — and this could be carried easily in a Lancaster.

With the results of these experiments, and a firm idea developing in his mind of the shape of the new bomb, Wallis went back to see the Director of an 'Operational Research' branch of one of the Ministries, Professor Patrick Blackett. One again, Sir Henry Tizard, who was shown the results of Wallis's experiments, went down to Weybridge to see the designer. When he left, Wallis had permission to use the huge water tank at Teddington, used in ship model trials. At one end of the tank he had a model of the Moehne Dam built. With the aid of both surface and underwater cameras he was able to follow the trajectory of small-scale bombs, as they skipped over the surface of the water, then follow them down underwater as they hit the face of the dam.

Nearly three years had passed by now, so Oberburgermeister Dillgardt need not have worried his Military authorities *quite* so soon.

Meanwhile back in Weybridge things were going well for Wallis. By a strange twist of fate, a gentleman named Lane came to see Wallis about one of his earlier ideas, which had nothing to do with blowing up dams. Wallis gave him the information he required, then told him of his latest idea. Lane was interested, and promised he would mention it to his boss when he got back to the Ministry of Defence. He did, with the result that Wallis got six half-size bombs made to his new design.

On the 4th December 1942, one of these bombs was fitted to a specially converted Wellington bomber and was taken on a test drop over the South Coast off Chesil Beach. Piloting the plane was Mutt Summers, Chief Test Pilot at Weybridge. Wallis acted as bomb aimer, lying flat on his tummy and peering through the bomb aimer's window in the nose of the aircraft. Summers flew low over the water, and Wallis released the bomb. The results were not good, for on impact with the water the casing was seen to crumble. On his return to Weybridge, Wallis had the other five casings strengthened. Next time they went out on a test drop all went well. It was decided to take a cine film of the next three drops. All were successful.

Armed with this cine film, Wallis once again headed for Whitehall. This time he got permission to design a full-size bomb. This was in early February 1943. Three months later the dams would be at their maximum level. Things had to accelerate if a target date in May was going to be met. What could he do? With the aid of Mutt Summers, Wallis got an interview with the Chief of Bomber Command, Air Marshal Sir Arthur Harris, with the object of getting his permission to use a Lancaster to try out the full-size bomb. They showed him their film of the tests, which now included cine of the Teddington trials. Harris promised them he would think it over and let them know.

Shortly after this interview, Wallis was summoned to Whitehall and told that the Prime Minister had granted permission for him to go all out to blow up the Ruhr Dams in May.

At last everything was working in Wallis's favour. But had they allowed him enough time? Could he perfect the bombs? Back in his office again, he tried to collect his thoughts. He had to battle with so many people over the past three years, but now it was all over: all he had to do was to perfect the bomb. It was up to Harris to provide the aircraft and aircrew.

Preparation

Air Vice Marshal the Hon. Ralph Cochrane had just taken over as Air Officer Commanding No.5 (Bomber) Group, with his Headquarters in Grantham. Two days later he was in Air Marshal Sir Arthur Harris's office, listening carefully as Harris explained Wallis's idea. This was to be one raid only, and none of the usual operations were to be cancelled. Everyone taking part in this Dams raid of Wallis's had to be picked from aircrew just finishing a tour of operations, volunteers who would take on one last raid.

It was Harris who, with Cochrane's approval, picked Wing Commander Guy Gibson to command the new squadron. This was to be a strange unit, born for the sole purpose of blowing up some dams in the Ruhr. But there was no time to waste in getting the unit knocked into shape for the raid. Back at Grantham again, Cochrane sent for Gibson.

At the age of 25, and with 173 operational trips to his credit, the DSO and bar, and the DFC, Guy Gibson was a short stocky man, with a handsome boyish face. He had just finished his last operation of the tour and was about to have some well earned leave when he was transferred to the HQ staff at Grantham. He was naturally disappointed at not being allowed to go on leave. Nevertheless he duly presented himself in Cochrane's office at the appointed time. He was then asked by AOC if he would mind doing one more operational trip. When he agreed, Cochrane told him he would be in charge of the operation, but that was all he could tell him about it for the present. Outside, Gibson wondered just what he had let himself in for. This must be something very special. Two days later he was called into Cochrane's office again, this time the AOC was not alone. With him was the CO of Scampton, Group Captain Charles Whitworth. Scampton was the home of No.57 Squadron, equipped with Lancasters.

The AOC introduced the two men, then told Gibson that the operation he had volunteered for was going to be a big one, one that would require an entire squadron of Lancasters; Whitworth was there because Gibson was going to use Scampton as a base for the squadron he was going to form. He added that the operation would not take place for at least eight weeks. This would give

Marshal of the Royal Air Force Sir Arthur Harris, G.C.B., O.B.E., A.F.C. A.O.C. Bomber Command 1942

Gibson a chance to form the squadron into an efficient unit, the best in the Group. The choice of aircrews would be left to Gibson, but he must only pick crews that were near the end of their operational tours. Each squadron in the group would probably be asked to give up some of their crews. It was up to Gibson to sort out the best.

What was the mission? This was the question Gibson wanted answered, but he was told by the AOC that he would learn 'in due course', though he *was* told to have his aircrews flying in four days time!

With this shattering piece of information, Gibson and Whitworth were dismissed. Outside in the corridor, Whitworth smiled at Gibson, who looked dazed. He knew the problems facing the new squadron commander. He wished him luck and said he would see him at Scampton in a couple of days, then as a parting shot said he would arrange accomodation at the base for Gibson and his men. The next two days were hardly long enough for Gibson. His first call was upstairs, to an office where he picked out some of the names of aircrew he wanted. It took him over an hour of hard work. Most of the men were on leave, but he knew them personally, and knew too that they would be disappointed if he left them off his list.

There were other crews to be found, for twenty new aircraft had to be manned. Picking bomber crews was not an easy job, but it was eventually done. Next stop was with the equipment officer. Here Gibson asked for ten aircraft to start with, the rest to follow in a few days. All the necessary equipment to keep them flying would also be needed, right down to the last 2 B.A. nut. The time soon went by, as Gibson went from room to room seeing various people, acquiring every last item required on a squadron, from toilet rolls to motor lorries. Everything was ordered, and delivery promised at Scampton by the following day.

The next day Gibson spent with the personnel officer, picking ground crews, orderly room staff, cooks, police, everyone in fact who went to make a squadron function. Then it was into the stationery office to order all the forms, requisitions, charge sheets, and so forth. The job seemed endless to Gibson, but although this was the first time he had had to do this sort of thing, he tackled it

Crew Teams required to keep a Lancaster flying

PETROL BOWSER & CREW

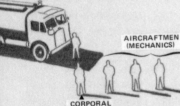

MOBILE WORKSHOP & CREW ▶

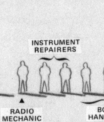

AIRCRAFTMEN
(MECHANICS)

FITTER
(ARMOURER)

INSTRUMENT
REPAIRERS

CORPORAL
MECHANIC

ENGINEER
OFFICER

ARMOURERS

RADIO
MECHANIC

BOMB
HANDLERS

FITTER

FLIGHT
CREW

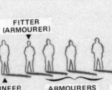

BOMB CREW

W.A.A.F. TRACTOR DRIVER

INSTRUMENT
REPAIRER

MECHANIC

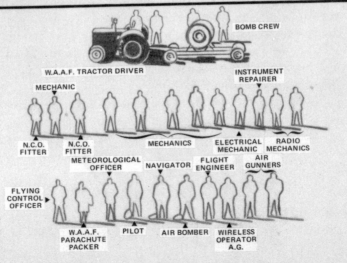

N.C.O.
FITTER

N.C.O.
FITTER

MECHANICS

ELECTRICAL
MECHANIC

RADIO
MECHANICS

METEOROLOGICAL
OFFICER

NAVIGATOR

FLIGHT
ENGINEER

AIR
GUNNERS

FLYING
CONTROL
OFFICER ▶

W.A.A.F.
PARACHUTE
PACKER

PILOT

AIR BOMBER

WIRELESS
OPERATOR
A.G.

CREW TEAMS REQUIRED TO KEEP A LANCASTER FLYING

in his usual thorough way. He would have been the first to admit he could not have done it without the help of everyone concerned at Headquarters. It took the whole of two days, with very little sleep for Gibson, for he worked well into the night making sure he had covered everything. But at last he was satisfied. He had formed his squadron. Due to the speed with which it had been organised, the department in Whitehall concerned with issuing squadron names and numbers, had not as yet managed to issue one to Gibson.

Next day Gibson went to Scampton, everything being finished as far as he was concerned at Headquarters. When he arrived, he headed for the officers' mess with his faithful black labrador 'Nigger'. Inside he found many old friends, mixed with several new faces he had not seen before. His own crew were there, and they greeted him with whoops of joy. A party was obviously in full swing. Nigger came in for a good deal of attention, too, for he liked his pint of beer. It was not long before Gibson was chatting away with everyone. It was mostly shop-talk — old targets, near misses, absent friends. Looking round him, Gibson noted with satisfaction that everyone was keen to be included in this, his new squadron. There was never a new outfit with so many experienced aircrew before. The number of DFCs and DSOs on the various tunics showed, to the casual observer that this was no ordinary squadron. These men between them had probably got more experience of bombing than any other squadron in the Royal Air Force.

They were a mixed bunch of nationalities, coming from Australia, America, Canada, New Zealand and Great Britain. From Gibson's old squadron, 106, there was three crews he knew well. Their Skippers were Hopgood, known as 'Hoppy' for short, was a good-looking fair haired English lad; Dave Shannon was from Australia and only twenty, but already he wore the ribbon of the DFC; and a young Flight Sergeant Burpee from Canada, who had just married a pretty English girl and was busily trying to find a house for her nearby.

There was the tall American from California, Melvyn Young, one of the fastest beer drinkers on the unit. He had the nick-name of 'Dinghy' because he had ditched twice and got away with it each time, saved by his rubber dinghy. He was a very efficient organizer and became Gibson's senior flight commander.

From 97 squadron came the New Zealander, Les Munro. Les was a quiet individual, but could always be counted on to do the right thing at the right time, a thoroughly reliable man, never known to get into a flap. With him was David Maltby, big but gentle, kind and thoughtful. David was a fine pilot.

There was Joe McCarthy from Brooklyn. Joe had come over to Britain to join the Royal Air Force before America entered the war. He was offered the chance of joining the United States Air Force when they later entered hostilities, but refused, preferring to stay in the RAF. He also was an ex-97 Squadron pilot, and a great friend of Les Munro. Weighing nearly 15 stone, he towered over the whole assembly. Once before he had tried to get into Gibson's squadron, but in spite of everything Gibson had done to get him in, they never managed it. Here he was at last, and very pleased about it.

There was Etonian Henry Maudslay. He was to be the other flight commander. Upon his shoulders would fall the organising of squadron training. Henry, a fine pilot, had come from 50 Squadron. A keen athlete, he had been a champion runner at school. He never drank too much.

Another Australian was Micky Martin of Sydney. Gibson had met Micky previously at an investiture at Buckingham Palace, they liked each other at once, and soon began talking shop. Martin had a profound belief that the lower you flew, the longer you lived. He had explained his theories to Gibson. The whole of Mickey's crew were Australian, including Jack Leggo, who became the new squadron navigation officer, Bob Hay who had been Group Bombing Leader, and was to do the same job for the squadron, Toby Foxley, Les Knight and Len Chambers.

The babble of conversation quieted down as Coles, a Canadian navigator, walked over to Gibson and asked him the question that everyone wanted to know. What was it all about? What was their mission? Gibson told them that they knew as much as he did, but he was going to hold a meeting of all aircrews the following morning at 9.30 a.m.

The time was well past midnight. Gibson's own crew had long

since gone to bed. Nigger was satisfied with his intake of beer, but as he weaved his weary way along the corridor with Gibson, heading for bed, he could no longer control his water works and left a trail zig-zagging behind him. He was a happy dog and went contentedly to bed with his tail between his legs.

Next morning the aircrews were assembled in the long briefing room over the station headquarters. The babble of conversation subsided as Gibson entered the room and walked up to the rostrum. With him was Nigger, by now quite sober. This room held many memories for Gibson and, looking around him now at the expectant faces, he thought back to his early days of the 1939-40 period, when he had sat as they were, awaiting briefing. His speech to them was short — it had to be for he knew as little as they did. What he was able to tell them was that they had been formed into a crack squadron to perform one raid on Germany which some people said would shorten the war. What or where the target was he did not know, but he did stress two points. First, discipline was essential. If he asked them to do something they were to do it without question. Second, it was of the utmost importance that they kept their mouths shut about their mission. Secrecy was essential on this raid. Anyone found breaking security would be severely dealt with. It was in their own interest, for their lives depended on it. Enquiring busybodies in the pub were to be told to mind their own business.

He told them it would take a little while to become organised and asked for everyone's help. Their first job was going to be the flight testing of their new aircraft. Flight commanders would be sorting the crews into flights and allocating them aircraft. He then asked young Bill Astell, 'Dinghy' Young's deputy flight commander to take his crew and photograph every lake and reservoir he could find in Britain, and have the photographs on his desk in thirty six hours. Gibson himself didn't realise the importance of the job, or its connection with his future raid, only that the AOC had made it Top Priority. Acting on inustructions, he explained that they had been chosen for the job as the only unit with time to spare.

His next bit of news for them was disappointing. The unit was to have no leave for at least two months, until after their

Gibson and members of 617 making a fuss of 'Nigger'

617 SQUADRON

PILOT	F/ENG	NAVIGATOR	W/OPTR	B/AIMER	MID-UPPER	REAR-GUNNER
Leader: W/C GIBSON, DSO, DFC	Sgt Pulford	P/O Taerum	F/L Hutchinson, DFC	P/O Spafford	F/L Trevor-Roper, DFM	F/S Deering

'A' Flight

PILOT	F/ENG	NAVIGATOR	W/OPTR	B/AIMER	MID-UPPER	REAR-GUNNER
S/L YOUNG, DFC	Sgt Horsfall	Sgt Roberts	Sgt Nichols	F/O MacCausland	Sgt Yeo	Sgt Ibbotson
F/L ASTELL, DFC	Sgt Kinnear	P/O Wile	Sgt Garshowitz	F/O Hopkinson	Sgt Garbas	Sgt Bolitho
F/L MALTBY, DFC	Sgt Hatton	Sgt Nicholson	Sgt Stone	P/O Fort	Sgt Hill	Sgt Simmonds
F/L SHANNON, DFC	Sgt Henderson	P/O Walker, DFC	F/O Goodale, DFC	F/S Sumpter	Sgt Jagger	P/O Buckley
F/L BARLOW	Sgt Whillis	P/O Burgess	F/O Williams	Sgt Gillespie	F/O Glinz	Sgt Liddell
P/O RICE	Sgt Smith	F/O MacFarlane	Sgt Gowrie	F/S Thrasher	Sgt Maynard	Sgt Burns
P/O OTTLEY	Sgt Marsden	F/O Barrett	Sgt Guterman	F/S Johnson	Sgt Tees	Sgt Strange
P/O DIVALL	Sgt Blake	F/O Warwick	Sgt Simpson	Sgt McArthur	Sgt Allatson	Sgt Murray
F/S BROWN	Sgt Feneron	Sgt Heal	Sgt Hewstone	Sgt Oancia	Sgt Buntaine	F/S McDonald
Sgt BYERS	Sgt Taylor	P/O Warner	Sgt Wilkinson	Sgt Whitaker	Sgt Jarvie	Sgt McDowell

Flight Bombing Leader: P/O FORT. Flight Gunnery Leader: F/O GLINZ. Flight Navigation Officer: F/O MACFARLANE.

'B' Flight

PILOT	F/ENG	NAVIGATOR	W/OPTR	B/AIMER	MID-UPPER	REAR-GUNNER
S/L MAUDSLAY, DFC	Sgt Marriott	F/O Urquhart	Sgt Cottam	F/S Fuller	F/O Tytherleigh	Sgt Burrows
F/L HOPGOOD, DFC	Sgt Bronnan	F/O Earnshaw	Sgt Minchin	F.S. Fraser	P/O Gregory, DFM	P/O Burcher, DFM
F/L MARTIN, DFC	P/O Whittaker	F/L Leggo, DFC	F/O Chambers	F/L Hay, DFC	P/O Foxlee, DFM	F/S Simpson
F/L MUNRO	Sgt Appleby	F/O Rumbles	Sgt Pigeon	Sgt Clay	Sgt Howarth	F/S Weeks
F/L McCARTHY	Sgt Ratcliffe	F/S MacLean	Sgt Eaton	Sgt Johnson	Sgt Batson	F/O Rodger
F/L WILSON	Sgt Johnson	F/O Rodger	Sgt Mieyette	P/O Coles	Sgt Payne	Sgt Hornby
P/O BURPEE	Sgt Pegler	Sgt Jaye	P/O Weller	Sgt Arthur	Sgt Long	F/S Brady
P/O KNIGHT	Sgt Grayston	F/O Hobday	Sgt Kellow	F/O Johnson	Sgt Sutherland	Sgt O'Brien
F/S TOWNSEND	Sgt Powell	P/O Howard	F/S Chalmers	Sgt Franklin	Sgt Webb	Sgt Wilkinson
F/S ANDERSON	Sgt Paterson	Sgt Nugent	Sgt Bickle	Sgt Green	Sgt Ewan	Sgt Buck

Flight Bombing Leader: F/O JOHNSON. Flight Gunnery Leader: F/O TYTHERLEIGH. Flight Navigation Officer: F/O URQUHART.

operation. This would normally have produced groans of discontent from his audience, but this time the crews were silent.

With a final reminder on discipline, both on the ground and in the air, he then handed the briefing over to Dinghy Young and Maudslay, who started the job of arranging offices, sorting the crews into flights, and allocating them flying lockers and crew rooms.

Gibson left them to it. He and Nigger departed for the bare cold office that was to be his for the next few months. Its only furnishings for the present were one table, one chair and one telephone. It was cold and damp, because no central heating had yet been turned on in the adjoining hangar. The windows were dirty, and generally it was not an encouraging sight. Even the brown lino on the floor was enough to discourage Nigger from stretching out by his master's desk. Instead he spread himself across the rough cocounut mat at the office door, and defied anyone to move him.

There was a young man over at Syerston by the name of Humphreys, who had failed his aircrew medical through bad eyesight, but was still mad about flying. He had been a businessman in peacetime, and everything from an orderly room clerk to assistant adjutant in war. Gibson knew him well, and realising the need for an adjutant, made a quick phone call through to Group and had Humphreys posted to his new unit, within twenty-four hours. Until he arrived, however, the job of forming the entire squadron fell on the shoulders of three people. These were Flight Sergeant Powell, the squadron's disciplinarian, Sergeant Hevron, boss of the orderly room, and a WAAF, who had come over from a satellite airfield because she had heard the new unit was short of typists. Gibson only knew her as Mary. She was plump and fair, and a very hard worker.

'Chiefy' Powell, who was a small dapper little man, didn't look anything like a disciplinarian at first sight. He had the happy knack of making whoever he was interviewing feel at ease. This brought out the best in them. Just at the moment he was interviewing 700 people, fitting them up with bunks and getting their sections organised. He was making a grand job of it, and, without realising it, laying the foundation of the spirit of the squadron with his friendly approach.

Sergeant Hevron in his orderly room was trying to deal with the paperwork that plagues every squadron in the RAF. As he was hampered by shortage of staff he worked over eighteen hours a day, dealing with new arrivals and the letters that kept pouring in. In the few minutes he did get free he went round to 57 Squadron, the other unit at Scampton, begging, borrowing and where necessary stealing, vital pieces of equipment for the new unit — items like parachutes, report forms and typewriters, which had not yet arrived.

So these three worked hard, getting the Squadron off to a good start, while up in his office Gibson sat in wonder at the way the unit was forming around him.

On the aircrew side, Jack Leggo and Bob Hay were sorting things out. Their problem was to get the aircraft flying. For this they required flight maps, compass keys, the testing of bomb sights, and the host of other jobs that went into getting those big four engined machines operational.

Then the men at the Ministry finally caught up with the new unit, giving it a squadron number. They were 617 Squadron, with the initials AJ — which were immediately painted on the sides of the aircraft in big red letters.

Meanwhile, Gibson was interviewing the aircrews, getting to know them. These were informal chats, so that they could all get acquainted. The captain of each crew would come in with his crew and introduce them to Gibson one at a time. They would discuss various things in the short conversation that followed, then out they would go to let in the next crew. From these meetings Gibson was able to tell if he thought they were the sort of crews he wanted on his squadron. He was carefully weighing every crew up, deciding if they met his standards. Some, not many, were unlucky. There was no shortage of crews at this stage of the war, so replacements came easily.

After three days of hard work, the aircraft were ready to start flying. This was one day ahead of the AOC's requested four day deadline.

That morning Chiefy Powell gathered all the ground personnel into one of the big hangars. Gibson drove into the centre of the hangar in his Humber shooting brake, got out and scrambled onto the roof of the vehicle. He signalled everyone to gather round informally, and gave them more or less the same speech he had given the aircrews. Once again his emphasis was on strict security. After he had spoken, he handed over to Charles Whitworth, the Station CO, who officially welcomed 617 Squadron to Scampton. Whitworth made an excellent speech. He never bored his listeners with trifles, and always kept their interest. Gibson wished he had a tape recorder with him, so that he could use some of Charles's material later in his own speeches.

Gibson's office did not look quite so bare now. The floor had a carpet on it — Could it have been scrounged by Sergeant Hevron? — and there were some very comfortable armchairs scattered about. Even Nigger approved. The heating was now on in the hangars and offices. Things were slowly getting organised.

That afternoon Gibson, with the aid of Humphreys his new adjutant (who had arrived that afternoon), made the first entry in the training report. It was short and to the point, stating that although:

The squadron had been formed on 20-3-43, full facilities for training had not been available until 25-3-43. On the 22-3-43 the squadron had been organised into two flights. Due to deficiencies such as starter trolleys for the aircraft and tool kits, parachutes and Mae Wests, only a limited number of training flights had been carried out.

Gibson had a conference in his office with Dinghy, Henry Maudslay, Jack Leggo and Bob Hay. The two flight commanders and their deputies sat around in armchairs, as Gibson explained the training flight programme. The AOC, he explained, wanted them to practice low flying. To start with he felt they should limit the height to 150 feet. This was done purely as a safety measure; he did not want the crews smashing into tree tops. In order not to be too much of a worry to the Observer Corps, he suggested they lay down ten practice routes. He would tell them later what sort of country they would be required to fly over. None of the routes should be over three hours duration to start with. Flying would be done both by day and night. A record of each navigator was to be kept. Then he asked if there were any problems. Jack said the maps the navigators had would not be any good for low flying.

Flying as low as they would be doing, it would be better to have roller maps. It meant that they would have to be made from existing maps by each navigator, but it could be done. Another problem for the navigator would be spotting landmarks. Would Gibson approve if the bomb-aimer was used as key-map reader, while the navigator stuck to his charts? The front gunner, flight engineer and mid-upper gunner could also act as spotters, looking for landmarks. This would mean four pairs of eyes helping the navigator. Gibson agreed to this, and many other constructive suggestions that were put forward.

Then the telephone rang on Gibson's desk. It was the AOC, who wanted to see Gibson right away at Group. Handing the meeting over to Dinghy, Gibson with Nigger by his side, went to his shooting brake. It was not long before he was motoring down the quiet country lanes, heading for Grantham.

At headquarters, Satterly, the SASO — Senior Air Staff Officer — met Gibson and told him he was to go south to meet a scientist who was working on Gibson's project. Stressing once again the need for secrecy, he said the man he was going to see would be able to answer most of his questions about the mission. He told Gibson to drive down to London, leave his car and driver at a certain main London station and board a train for Weybridge. Whatever he did, he must not let his driver know where he was going. It was all very 'cloak and dagger', but not without cause. Should the enemy get the slightest hint of the object of 617 Squadron's mission, the defences on the dams would most certainly be increased. As it was getting near the time when the dams would be at their fullest, somebody might take Oberburgermeister Dillgardt's warning more seriously, should they be put on the track by German agents in Britain.

When Gibson alighted at Weybridge station, he looked round him for some sign of recognition. He had simply been told that 'someone' would meet him. It turned out to be his old friend Mutt Summers, Chief Test Pilot at Vickers. Gibson had gone to Mutt for an interview just after he had left school and asked him for a job as a test pilot. The answer he got sent him into the RAF to get some experience and training. So here he was again, the same big handsome Mutt. They both crammed into Mutt's little Fiat and he drove for quite a way without either of them saying a word. When, after what seemed to Gibson a lifetime, they pulled into the drive of an old country house, a sentry came out and checked their passes. Then on up the drive they went, to come to a final stop outside the front door. Here again passes were checked, this time a little more closely, for Gibson was asked for the special pass he had been given by the SASO at Group that morning. After a final scrutiny by two burly policemen, they were allowed to pass. Walking through a maze of corridors they ended up in front of a large iron door, with more guards on duty. They both went through the same procedure as before. Satisfied, one of the guards opened the iron door, and they both passed through.

Inside, the lights were bright. After walking through the dim corridors for so long, it was a little while before Gibson's eyes became accustomed to the room. He found himself standing in what looked like some kind of laboratory. Coming towards them with hand outstretched was a tall, thin, elderly man, wearing thick horn-rimmed glasses, with a mop of white curly hair. He was a pleasant looking man, rather quiet, more like a country vicar than the scientist he was. It was of course Barnes Wallis. He came forward and greeted Gibson with a broad smile, and the eyes behind those horn-rimmed glasses twinkled as they saw the look of bewilderment on Gibson's face. Mutt introduced the two men, then Wallis, looking round carefully to make sure there were no spies about, asked Gibson if he knew the reason for his visit? He was told no. Wallis asked if Guy had any idea what the target was, but was answered once again, no. This seemed to take Wallis aback, for he had expected Gibson to come more or less fully briefed to this meeting. Instead, it was Gibson who was expecting Wallis to brief him. This was not possible, however, for security reasons. Wallis was not allowed to mention the target to anyone except those on a list that he had in his desk drawer. At the moment Gibson was not on the list. It was a ridiculous situation, and Wallis was the first to break through it, telling Gibson not to worry, they would show him what they could. Without mentioning the target, it was going to be very difficult.

Wallis explained his theories to Gibson, explaining vaguely that there were in existence in enemy territory certain objectives which

B

were military targets and very vulnerable to air attack. To destroy these objectives however needed a vast amount of explosives placing in the correct spot with a high degree of accuracy. This was not going to be easy. To place the explosives was the problem. This could not be done from a high flying aircraft, as sufficient accuracy could not be achieved. This in Wallis's view, left only one alternative — a low flying aircraft. There had been no aircraft capable of carrying the necessary load — until the Lancaster came on the scene. Whoever piloted that aircraft on this special mission would have to be able to fly a Lancaster low over water. When the explosive was released, and because of its specially shaped cannister, it would bounce along the surface of the water towards the correct spot on the target. It was like being at the seaside, skimming flat pebbles over the water — only this was no holiday!

Gibson's mind was reviewing all sorts of possible targets — the *Tirpitz*, U-boat pens, dry docks and many others. It is doubtful if he thought of the correct one.

Wallis could see the keen look of interest on Gibson's face, and went on telling him of the difficulties that had to be overcome. Then he motioned Guy to a couple of chairs that had been placed at one end of the laboratory, telling him they had some film to show him. They both sat down facing a white screen, while Mutt turned out the lights and switched on a projector. The title came flickering up, it was *Most Secret Trial Number One*. After this, an aircraft came on the screen. It was a Wellington bomber, but its bomb doors had been removed and there was a strange device suspended underneath in the bomb bay. The plane dived low over the water of what appeared to be an estuary. Suddenly some form of cannister was released, which seemed to glide slowly down to the water, hitting it with a large splash sending spray flying in all directions. Then the object came into view again, making several bounces along the surface, until it finally settled in the water and disappeared from sight. All this time the aircraft flew at the same height above the water, gradually pulling ahead of the 'bouncing' bomb. There were several shots like that on the film, each obviously taken at a different time, but in each instance the end result was the same.

Gibson's face was a picture when Mutt turned the lights on

again. Wallis's eyes started to twinkle again, for he could understand the young pilot's feelings. He went on to explain that the film they had been watching showed only quarter scale bombs. He feared that there would be problems with the much larger ones which Gibson and his pilots would be carrying. But that was his problem, and he hoped he could solve it in time.

Gibson asked if any of the large bombs had been made yet. He was told they were in production, and that, all being well, the first one would be delivered in about a week's time. Of course it also meant a rush modification programme on the Lancasters, which Messrs A.V. Roe were carrying out, working day and night. Bomb doors had to be taken off and special fitting put on. There were changes to the airframe to be made, the mid-upper gun turret had to be removed and some of the heavy armour plating taken out. This cut down the weight of the aircraft and so enabled the bombload to be that little bit more.

The next question Wallis asked Gibson was: 'Could you fly at a speed of 220 miles an hour at 150 feet above water, after pulling out of a dive from 2000 feet, and then be able to drop a bomb accurately within a few feet?'

Gibson was not too sure about this, but he said that he would give it a try and let Wallis know the results. Wallis was worried about the outcome. If Gibson and his men could not do this, the whole operation would have to be abandoned. Low flying was dangerous enough in daylight, as far too many accidents had proved. The Dams raid had to be done at night.

The briefing drew to an end with Wallis saying how sorry he was that he could not let Gibson into the secret of the target, but it could not be done. Perhaps Group would lift the veil for him a little when he got back. One thing Gibson did know now, was the the type of weapon — the bouncing bomb — he would be using on his raid. So with a hearty farewell handshake from Wallis, Mutt escorted Gibson out along the long corridors and into the fresh air again. Outside, Mutt's little white Fiat was standing where they had left it. He and Gibson squeezed back into it, the latter still in rather a daze after seeing the film. He was soon asking Mutt innumerable questions, and the journey back to the station did not seem to take so long as it had when they came.

He hardly noticed the train journey back to London, and when he got back to the Station, and Nigger peered at him through the window of his car, barking and wagging his tail, Gibson was making mental notes on future training flights. Now he knew the type of training to give his pilots.

Back at Scampton, he went with Nigger straight to his own office, only to find all aircrews out on practice flights. He had so many things he wanted to think out, he decided to go for a walk. Nigger was the only one who gained anything from the walk however. He came back with a rabbit. Gibson still had his problems. How long would it be before Group told him the target?

Next day he had another conference in his office with several of the boys, including the two flight commanders and their deputies. He explained the flying problems to them, but said nothing about the weapon itself.

Dinghy was the first one to comment. Flying in moonlight was not going to be easy in this country, neither was there time to sit around and wait for a good moonlit night. The only answer he could think of, was to simulate night-flying conditions. How could this be done? Harry suggested dark glasses, but was told they were no good, as you could not see the flying instruments.

This was where the Americans could help, for the AAF had just brought out a new synthetic method of simulating night flying. They sprayed the inside of all the aircraft's windows with a special blue transparent paint. The aircrew all wore yellow glasses, and because the colours were complementary, the result was the image of a perfect moonlight night. The instruments could be read easily, likewise the navigator's maps. In fact, once in the aircraft, it was impossible to believe that you were flying in broad daylight. Dinghy had heard about this from one of his American friends, and suggested to Gibson that they give it a try.

Gibson was in full agreement, and told him to contact the Senior Air Staff Officer (SASO) at Group right away to see what he could do about getting the Lancaster fitted up with this type of simulation. Five minutes later Dinghy was back with the news that if they sent three aircraft down to Ford right away, they would be given top priority. The aircraft were despatched.

Jack Leggo came up with a navigational problem. Some of the

navigators were finding it hard to navigate at low altitutde, as they were not used to it. Could they have extra practice? Some of them were already doing eight hours a day flying, but they could double up with navigators who were having less trouble.

Several other problems came up ... special tracer bullets for the gunners ... the use of the range from dusk to dawn ... flame-floats ... Poor Hutch, who was in charge of the radio operators, wondered where he fitted into it all. Gibson told him not to worry, he had not been forgotten: his turn would come. In one respect the Squadron had become too keen. The Provost Marshal had been to see Gibson with reports of dangerous low flying. Various reports had come to them from the police, other aerodromes and courting couples. The aircrews themselves had been finding leaves and even small branches of trees stuck in the engine radiators of the aircraft. Gibson knew that they had to get some low flying practice, but some pilots were making this the excuse for stupid stunts. Gibson tore them off a strip. Any more reports from the Provost Marshal, and the pilot concerned would be severely dealt with. Then he told them that in half an hour's time he was going to do some trials to see if the mission was possible at all.

Collecting his crew, Guy walked across the dispersal and climbed into his aircraft, 'G-for-George'. The engines burst into life as he pressed their starter buttons and after a brief engine check the big machine trundled forward on the perimeter track and headed for the main runway, stopping at the end of the runway until clearance for take-off was received from the control tower. A green light flashed from the tower. Gibson pushed the throttles fully open and the great machine started to move down the runway. Gradually the speed increased until power could be felt on the control surfaces, then Gibson lifted the tail off the deck. The throbbing vibrations ceased, and the aircraft was airborne, climbing slowly.

Gibson headed the machine for Derwent Water, near Sheffield. This was the perfect lake over which to try and meet Wallis's requirements, for it was surrounded by the Pennines, which shielded the water from the wind, thus leaving it always calm. At last it lay ahead of them. Remembering what Wallis had said, he took the aircraft to 2,000 feet, then dived down to level out at 150 feet above the water. To make things a little more realistic, Gibson had had a few flame floats fitted to the aircraft. One of these he released when he thought the time was right. Suddenly the hills were coming up at the aircraft, and pulling back on the control column, Guy climbed the aircraft up again to 2,000 feet, turning the machine, to come in low over the water once again. This he did several times until dusk, when a low mist developed over the water, making it almost impossible to see the surface of the lake. He had one last try at a mock attack. This time he almost ploughed into the lake. Quickly pulling the control column back, Gibson just saved the machine. P/O. 'Spam' Spafford, who was in the bomb-aimer's compartment lying flat on his tummy peering out through his big domed window, was heard to ejaculate 'Christ!' This meant it was dangerous indeed, for nothing usually worried Spam. That was enough for Guy. He headed the machine back to Scampton, the problem of keeping a constant height above the water unsolved.

When they had landed, and were back in his office, Gibson explained what he had tried to prove with the test. Firstly he had wanted to find out if he could keep a constant given height and airspeed. He was satisfied about airspeed, but not about the height, which remained a problem.

The crew wanted to know why was it so important to have to fly at a set height and speed — for Gibson had not yet told them about the weapon. All he told them was that the scientist he had visited had asked if he could do just that. He had said he would have a try, and if it could be managed, then the raid was on. If he could not, then the raid was off. After these trials, he felt confident that the raid could be made, but the problem of height still worried him. How can you fly at a constant height without the altimeter? Clearly the instrument was not accurate enough at low level. But what could be used in its place? This was the problem he asked them all to think about.

Next morning he was up bright and early, but still the problem remained. After breakfast he went into his office and had just sat down when the telephone rang. It was Group. The AOC wanted to see him right away.

When Gibson was shown into Cockrane's office, he noticed three large packing cases on the floor. The AOC came forward to greet him with a smile, offering him a screwdriver. He told Guy that he was not going to tell him where the targets were, or what they were, because he had not yet got clearance; he was going to show him three models. Wallis had told the AOC that Gibson obviously could not train his crews unless he knew what they would be attacking. But only he out of the whole squadron must know the secret.

The two men worked with a screwdriver each, releasing the screws that held down the lids of the boxes. Each box was marked 'Very Fragile'.

One by one the lids were removed, and inside, perfect in every detail down to the last tree, were models of three dams. Gibson heaved a sigh of relief, for at the back of his mind was the idea that the squadron had been formed to sink the German battleship *Tirpitz*. This was a different proposition altogether. As he looked more closely at the models, Gibson realised that they were very large dams. Two of them were of similar construction, but the third was slightly different.

Now the AOC was talking to him again, telling him to go back and see Wallis, now that he had seen the targets. He was to report back to Cochrane on his return. Everything was falling into place now. *This* was why Wallis was worried about height and speed over water.

Back again with Wallis, Gibson was feeling a little more relieved. Wallis's first question was about the trials. How had he got on? Could it be done? Reassuring him that they had been successful in daylight, Guy explained the problem of maintaining the correct height at dusk. Wallis asked him if he could see the end of the lake coming, Gibson said he could. Wallis got out of his desk a file with words Operation 'Upkeep' in bold black letters on the front. At the top and bottom of the file stamped in red were the words *Top Secret*.

Wallis explained to Gibson the reason why such accurate bombing was required. He told him there was basically two types of dams — Vault and Barrage. The type he was going to bomb was the latter. Barrage dams are known as gravity dams and hold back

TWO TYPES OF DAMS

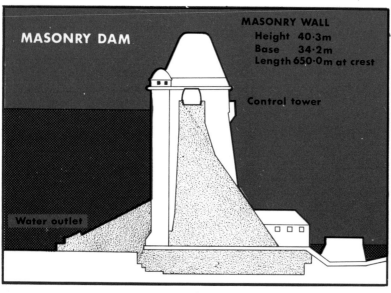

MASONRY DAM

MASONRY WALL
Height 40·3m
Base 34·2m
Length 650·0m at crest

Control tower

Water outlet

Point of release a

Möhne and Eder Dams

Ennepe, Sorpe and Lister Dams

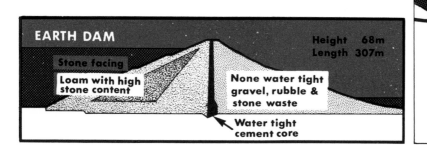

EARTH DAM

Height 68m
Length 307m

Stone facing

Loam with high stone content

None water tight gravel, rubble & stone waste

Water tight cement core

Showing the two types of dams and attacks

TWO TYPES OF ATTACK

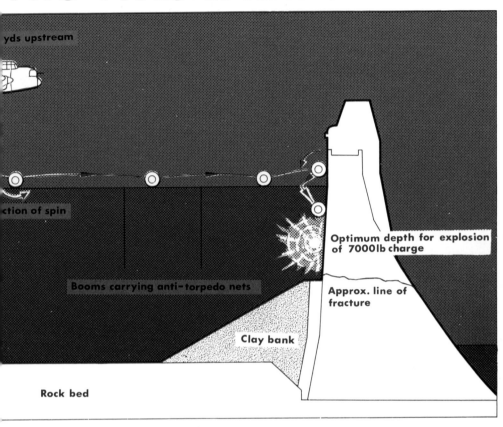

yds upstream

ction of spin

Booms carrying anti-torpedo nets

Clay bank

Rock bed

Optimum depth for explosion of 7000lb charge

Approx. line of fracture

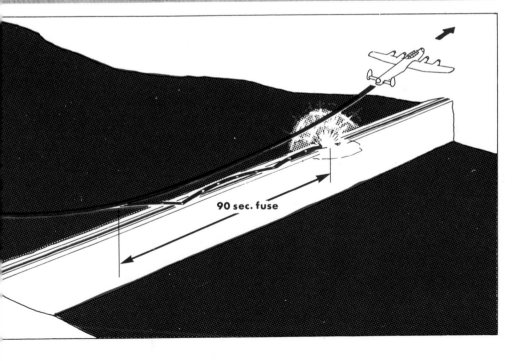

90 sec. fuse

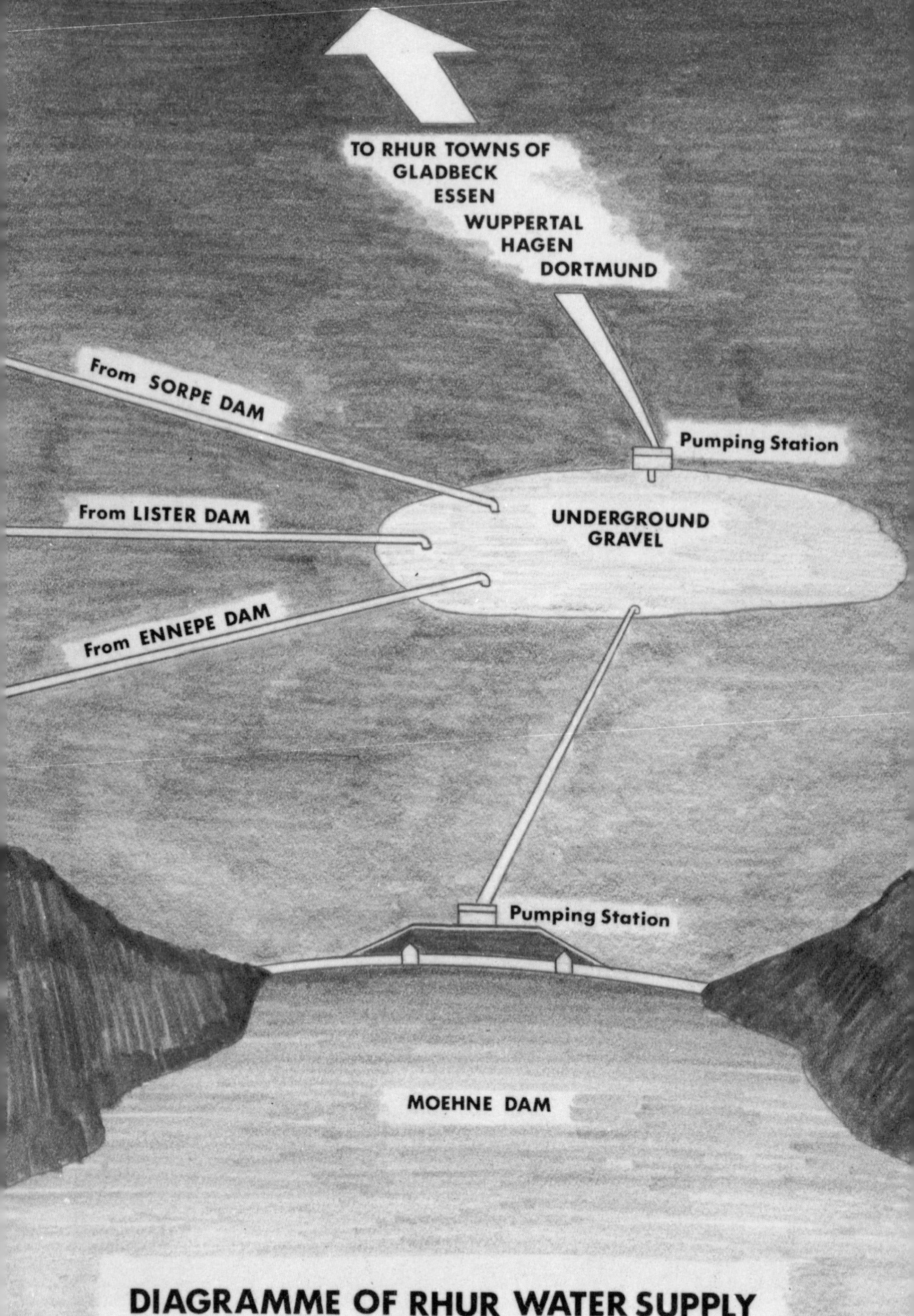

TO RHUR TOWNS OF
GLADBECK
ESSEN
WUPPERTAL
HAGEN
DORTMUND

From SORPE DAM

Pumping Station

From LISTER DAM

UNDERGROUND
GRAVEL

From ENNEPE DAM

Pumping Station

MOEHNE DAM

DIAGRAMME OF RHUR WATER SUPPLY SYSTEM

the water by their weight. Here again there were two types, concrete and earth, the former made of solid concrete and masonry, standing 150 feet high, with a base 140 feet thick. The earth type dams were virtually what the name suggested — great sloping mounds of earth with a watertight concrete core. The dams Gibson had seen in model form in the AOC's office were in the Ruhr Valley.

Gibson, who was now listening intently, asked why they could not be bombed with ordinary bombs. Wallis laughed. Everyone asked that question. It could not be done. When the Germans bombed Britain, people dived into shelters with only three feet of concrete protecting them — and survived. The Ruhr dams were 150 feet thick. Wallis went into the theory of how it could be tackled — ideas that Oberburgermiester Dillgardt would have recognised.

Wallis went on to explain the intricate method the Germans had of getting water from two rivers, the Ruhr and the Rhine. The Ruhr Valley was the most highly industrialized area in the whole of Germany. Heavy industry relied on two things, water and electricity for survival. Take away the water and you stopped industry. The two mains dams in the Ruhr Valley to attack would be the Moehne and Sorpe, with the Lister and Ennepe dams of secondary importance. Although these last two were smaller, they were still vital to the water supply. The water supply system for the Ruhr was a complex one. The river itself was not big enough to supply enough water to meet the demands of industry. By far the largest amounts of the area's water came from underground, a stratum of water-bearing sand and gravel, rather like a giant sponge. Because industry was demanding more and more water, there was in the early days a fear that this area might become dried out. To prevent this, the Germans built a series of dams up in the mountains which could collect and store the winter rain. This would slowly be fed into the sand and gravel area, thus acting as a controlled supply. Should it be necessary, the Rhine could also be tapped. All in all, this was quite a complicated water system. The plan that Wallis unfolded to Gibson was simply to breach these two most important dams with his bombs, releasing their water. This would dry up the main source of supply, and

Diagram of Rhur water system

hopefully the demand would be impossible to meet, causing the heavy industries to stop production. A side product of the enterprise would be the damage done by flooding. It was thought this would be considerable.

The third dam Guy had seen in Cochrane's office in model form was the Eder, which was about 60 miles away to the south-east of the Moehne. The purpose of this dam was twofold, first to prevent winter flooding of the lower Weser River and provide additional water for the Mittelland Canal, second to supply hydro-electric power. This dam did not supply water for either domestic or industrial use, neither was it tied into the Ruhr system. It was a large dam, however, larger than the Moehne, holding back 202 million tons of water. The Moehne dam held back 140 million tons of water. Between them, the Moehne and Sorpe held about 76 per cent of all the Ruhr Valley water supply.

Wallis went on to explain how, with the aid of scale models of a dam, he had exploded small charges of explosives in a series to gauge the correct amount required to blow out the dam walls. He showed Gibson photographs of the experiments to prove his points. Then, from the models, Wallis went to the real thing. He found that Birmingham County Council had just built an extension on to one of their old dams in the Welsh hills. They were due to demolish the old dam wall, so Wallis asked if he could do it for them with his new bomb. He had already calculated the exact amount of explosive he would need. This dam in the Rhayader Valley was about one fifth the size of the Moehne. On this occasion, Wallis primed a bomb and carefully lowered it down the face of the dam. Having connected it up with an electrical detonator, they then played out the cable until they were a safe distance away. Saying a small prayer, Wallis pushed the plunger down and hoped. The valley echoed with the sound of the muffled explosion, and a great white plume of spray went up into the air. The concrete wall of the dam crumbled. A large hole about 15 by 12 feet appeared, and the water rushed out and into the valley below.

Gibson saw the results of all these experiments in photographs. He was convinced that Wallis had the right idea. After his first meeting with Wallis, he had developed a great faith in this man of

Moehne Dam prior to the attack

science. Now some of Wallis's enthusiasm was rubbing off on to Guy. Could it be that the results of this raid really would bring the end of war nearer? It was certainly worth a try.

But Wallis was talking again. He said that so far his calculations had been correct about the bomb. However, this did not mean that they were correct when it came to the full size bomb, for so far he had only used scale models of the real thing. They would soon know the results. Some trials had been set for the 16th of March. If the results of these were good, then the raid was on. A.V. Roe would be modifying twenty-five Lancaster B.III Specials for the raid. The work of converting these aircraft was rather involved, so they would be working flat-out at Manchester, and it all had to be completed within a month.

Guy wanted to know why it was so urgent to complete all this work on such a tight schedule.

The answer was that the period 13th-19th May was the time when the dams would be at their fullest. Each day now for some weeks past, they had been photographed by a reconnaissance Mosquito aircraft. The water level had been noted on each photograph, and the defences of the dams carefully scrutinized. Slowly the water was rising — the level now was 12 feet from the top. The correct time for an attack was when the water was 4 feet from the top. It just happened that the water would reach this level during a moon period — which would be useful for the aircrews. Each bomb would have to be placed carefully against the wall of the dam, so that when it sank it would roll down the dam's face. A hydrostatic fuse was fitted to the bomb which would detonate at a depth of 30 feet.

Wallis told Gibson that his ordinary bombsight would be useless on this mission, because the bombs had to be released before the aircraft reached the dam wall. The point of release would be approximately 1,200 to 1,350 feet before the wall. The bomb would be released spinning in opposition to the direction in which the aircraft was travelling. It would skip along the top of the water, until it came up against the 4 foot exposed wall of the dam. Then it would roll up the wall, and this is where the spin of the bomb would come into its own, for when the bomb bounced off the wall, the direction of spin would force the bomb back against the wall of the dam, allowing it to roll down the face of the wall. The fuse would do the rest.

Should the bomb be released too early, the momentum of the spin would be lost. If released too late it could strike the parapet and explode. This could cause damage to the aircraft, if it did not completely destroy it. With the bomb dropped correctly, even though there would be a large explosion, the aircraft would be protected by the dam itself. Not only that, the aircraft would be at least 100 yards away when the bomb went off.

The problems, as far as Gibson was concerned, were twofold. How to keep to the correct height above the black water, and how to get the correct range for dropping the bomb. With these two problems in his mind, Gibson returned to Grantham and reported to the AOC.

Back at Headquarters, Gibson told Cochrane of his problems. The AOC listened thoughtfully, then told Guy he would put them in the hands of the 'Back-room Boys' to see what they could come up with. The main thing at the moment was to get the squadron efficient at low flying.

Now the targets were known to Gibson, he could plan a similar route to the one they would be taking over Germany on the actual raid. The converted aircraft had also been flown back from Ford, and the synthetic night-flying equipment was found to be very effective, so effective in fact, that it made the aircrews feel very sleepy. It was a strange feeling, to be flying along under conditions of night, when it was in fact broad daylight. Everyone tried it, and all came to the same conclusion: it was perfect.

The new routes that Gibson had the Navigation Officer prepare took them over lakes, which made good landmarks. Flying so low was going to require a high degree of accuracy on the part of the navigator. All other crews in the squadron could get their practice in during daylight, thanks to this new idea of the simulated night-flying aircraft. This was not possible for Gibson's own crew, however, for the Skipper was always so busy during the day that they could only get their practice during the late afternoon or evening. Gibson expected to hear moans from his crew about all the beer they were missing. Instead he found they actually preferred it, for it meant that they not only saved their money, but gained the bonus of night-flying experience as well. But it was hard on Gibson, for he had to run the squadron during the day, and because he was himself going to lead the raid, had also to become proficient at low-level night-flying.

One day towards the end of April, Gibson was seated alone in his office with Nigger stretched out asleep on the carpet, when there was a knock on his door. The visitor, a Wing Commander Dann, had just arrived from London — with the answer to Gibson's bombsight problem. It was simplicity itself. He had carefully studied the photographs of the dams, noting that both the Moehne and Eder had two towers along the dam's wall, 600 feet apart. From his pocket he drew out a sketch, of a simple bombsight. Within half an hour the instrument section sent a prototype of the new bombsight over. It consisted simply of a piece of plywood shaped in a triangular form. From each of two corners protruded a nail, in the other corner was an eyepiece, a simple peephole. Compared with modern bombsights it was laughable. Gibson took it up in 'G-for-George' to see if it worked, and it turned out to be the answer to his prayer. Wing Commander Dann went back to the Ministry of Aircraft Production in London a happy man.

Having given instructions to Bob Hay to get all the bomb-aimers to make new bombsights on the model of Dann's prototype, Gibson was anxious to see how his crews would make out on the range. The next few days showed that, with the new sights, accuracies to within three yards could be recorded. A competition spirit developed, with the winner buying the drinks. Now the only problem remaining for Gibson was how to maintain a constant height above the top of the water.

After three weeks of low flying, both day and night, the squadron soon became experts. All navigators were becoming very familiar with this type of point-to-point low-flying. If Gibson had asked them to find a tree in the middle of England, they reckoned they could do it.

Gibson now felt the time had come to start drawing up the route for the raid. To do this he wanted to consult a fellow pilot by the name of Charles Pickard. He knew more about the light flak defences in the coastal areas of Holland and Belgium than any

The bomb sight

other living soul, with the exception of the enemy. Pickard's fame came from a film made by the Crown Film Unit called *Target for Tonight*, in which he acted as the captain of a Wellington bomber, 'F' for Freddie. He was in fact a very good pilot with many sorties to his credit.

Pickard had his own special map of the coastline. On it, marked in red, were all the heavily defended areas along the coast, and there were a lot of them. But a way could be found through them which did not pass within a mile of the guns. Pickard showed the route to Gibson, who returned to Scampton and with the aid of Charles Whitworth, Scampton's CO and the SASO set about plotting the routes to the target, and a route similar to the real thing for practice purposes. The course took them out over the North Sea, then across the Dutch Islands and into Holland. On the practice course they went out into the North Sea, but doubled back and came in over the Wash, simulating the approach over the Dutch Islands. Picking turning points that would show up well in moonlight, the course to the target was settled. Substitute turning points for the practice run were also chosen, each one because of its similarity to the real thing. The river Trent was the substitute for the Rhine, the Cotswolds for the Ruhr hills, Uppingham Reservoir for the Moehne, and Colchester Lake for the Eder. There was a point on the Norfolk coast that was exactly like that of Egmond, the chosen gap in the German defences on the Hook of Holland, even down to a windmill. So now it was nearly all settled. The target route was fixed, so was the practice one. All that remained was to solve that irritating problem of height.

After this meeting, when Gibson was once again alone in his office, he sent for Jack Leggo and gave him the practice course with instructions to get all crews so used to it that they could do it blindfolded.

By now there was developing on the squadron a feeling of solidarity. The *esprit de corps* of the unit was amazing. Of their own free will, both aircrew and ground crew had set about making the squadron's offices and hangars, mess and billets presentable, painting doors and windows, making flower gardens, and generally cleaning up the place.

Early on April 15th, on the quiet stretch of sands at Parkstone

in the Thames Estuary stood a little group of people. The full-size
bombs were about to be tested. The group consisted of Wallis,
several men from the Ministry, Gibson and Bob Hay. The tide was
just on the ebb, and at that particular part of the estuary the
beach was quite shallow. The idea was that when the bomb had
been dropped, the group could wade out and inspect the casing of
the weapon for damage. Just at this moment all faces were looking
eastwards, the direction from which the aircraft would approach.
Two white marker buoys had been set out in the estuary,
representing the two towers on the wall of the dam. They were the
aiming point. Piloting the bombing aircraft was 'Shorty' Longbottom, of Vickers.

Standing there waiting, straining their ears to hear the sound of
aero engines, the little group looked at their watches. He should be
coming any second now. Then they heard him, or rather them, for
out of the sun came two Lancasters flying side by side, steady and
low. The other aircraft would be taking movie film, and another
cine camera had been set up on the beach. The aircraft came
thundering up over the water. Then the bomb was released and
very slowly separated from the aircraft. Time seemed to stand still,
everything seemed to be working in slow motion. With a great
white splash which seemed to reach out for the aircraft like giant
fingers coming up from the water, the bomb landed. Seconds later
fragments could be seen hurtling through the white spray. The
casing had shattered. A glum silence descended on the little group,
broken by Wallis saying that he would be holding another test
later that day.

By working hard in the hangars at Manston without a break, the
men managed to get the second test bomb's casing strengthened
ready for the late afternoon's trials. Once again the group
assembled on the beach awaiting the roar of aircraft engines. Over
they came again, this time with Mutt Summers at the controls of
the weapon-carrying aircraft. The weapon was released and
descended with the same slow motion characteristic of the
previous one. Up went the great white plume again, with
fragments of the casing once again flying in all directions.

For Wallis it must have been heartbreaking. The others felt

sorry for him. All parties concerned returned whence they had come.

Still the problem of height worried Gibson, and all sorts of things were tried to find an answer, from trailing wire out below the aircraft with a weight attached, to carefully measured low flying runs over the lakes. Pilots would fly at what they thought was the correct height, while instruments checked to show how far out they were. This idea was abandoned, however, because it was impossible to judge correct height at night in this way.

Gibson was sent for by the SASO at Grantham. On his arrival he met Ben Lockspeiser from the MAP. The answer to measuring height accurately at night had been found, as Lockspeiser explained, by fitting a spotlight to each wing of the aircraft and pointing the beams towards the water so that they converged into one spot when the aircraft was the correct height. The pilot lowered the aircraft until the two spots met, knowing he was then at his correct height. Lockspeiser explained that it was not a new idea and in fact had been used in the First World War. Simplicity was again the answer, as with the bombsight. When Guy returned to Scampton and explained the idea to the boys, Spam told him he'd had the same idea the night before when Terry and he had gone to a theatre. A girl had come onto the stage to do a dance and two spotlights had shone on her from the back of the auditorium.

The main thing now was to get an aircraft down to Farnborough to have two Aldis lamps fitted. Gibson detailed Henry Maudslay to fly his aircraft down. Farnborough gave the job top priority, and he was back the next day. The same night the idea was tried out. Gibson stood on out on the aerodrome and watched the big black Lancaster approaching over the end of the runway. Then the two lamps were switched on, and Henry at the controls brought the aircraft down until the two beams met and formed one spot on the runway. He was able to hold the spot steady, for the beams had been pointed slightly to port and he could see them by peering out of his window. When he landed, Guy asked him what he thought. Henry only had one suggestion, to point the beams to the other side of the aircraft and let his navigator tell him when he was at the correct height. He found it rather difficult to concentrate on flying the aircraft on instruments and keep looking out of the window to see if his height was right.

Next day, technicians started fitting the modification to the other aircraft; and soon the whole unit was able to fly at the required 150 feet above water, to within two feet. Gibson's problem was now solved, but as he watched his aircraft on practice night-flights, he could not help wishing for a different solution. He thought what the German gunners would do, presented with illuminated targets like these. So the answer to one problem had in itself brought another, for which there was no answer.

There was now only one remaining problem to be solved -- that of the weapon itself. Wallis was getting near the end of his tether, for each practice drop proved a failure. Time after time they strengthened the casings, each time without success. Then one day the answer came. Again it was simple. The dropping height of the weapon was reduced, the speed of the aircraft slightly increased. Wallis had spent many hours studying the thousands of feet of cine film. From this he had worked out that the weapon should be dropped from 60 feet instead of 150 feet, and the aircraft's speed should be 232 mph.

One day a Mosquito aircraft landed at Scampton and taxed round to 617 Squadron's dispersal. Out of it clambered Shorty Longbottom. He went to Gibson's office with orders to fly him to Weybridge. Within a few minutes the little aircraft was airborne and heading for Brooklands with Guy seated beside Shorty in the navigator's seat. As soon as they landed, they went straight to Wallis's office. Gibson noticed how tired and drawn he looked. Nevertheless, a smile of welcome came over his face on seeing Gibson again. He explained to Guy how they had at last solved their problem, but he now had to ask Guy if his crews could fly lower than their practising height. Would it be possible for them to fly at *sixty* feet?

Flying at this height left little margin for error, as Guy well knew. The only answer he could give Wallis was that they would have a crack at it that night and see how they made out. He would let him know the following morning.

Shorty flew him back to Scampton, where he immediately set about getting the spotlights altered to converge at 60 feet. When it got dark, David Maltby was the first to take off and test the new height adjustments. He found it possible, but felt that he did not dare sneeze. Guy was the next one to try. He found it just as easy to keep the aircraft at 60 feet as at 150 feet. But there was no margin for error.

Meanwhile the reconnaissance pictures showed the steady rise of the water level in the dams. Now it was only 10 feet from the top, and it was early May. As soon as it was 4 feet from the top, Gibson and his crews would be ready to go, and Oberburgermeister Dillgardt's fear would become a reality.

On the 1st of May, Guy had phoned Wallis and told him the new height could be managed. Wallis invited Guy down to the next set of trials, due to take place a day or two later. These trials, flown by Mutt, were a complete success. Wallis, overcome by joy, danced like a schoolboy by the water's edge. Gibson also showed his relief. Both of them threw their hats in the air with glee. Mutt, who was banking his aircraft to see how the weapon behaved, spotted two little figures jumping and dancing about on the edge of the beach below. He knew he did not need to look for the bomb. It worked.

Now the go-ahead was given to the ordnance factories to proceed with the manufacture of the bombs for the raid. The people in the factories worked day and night to get them out. At the same time the new aircraft began to come through from A.V. Roe; Roy Chadwick and his team had been working day and night, too, on what they knew as 'Type 464 Provisioning' of the Mark III Lancaster. The modifications to the aircraft were considerable, and when Gibson saw these new modified aircraft land at Scampton for the first time he found it hard to belive they were Lancasters. When they had finally come to rest at 617 Squadron's dispersals, and the engineering officer Flight Lieutenant Capel — known as 'Capable' Capel — got inside one, he found all sorts of new gadgets. It took a few days to deliver the new aircraft to the squadron, and as they came in each one was allocated to a crew. They were of course brand new and each pilot took a great pride in his new plane. Gibson even heard one pilot giving his bomb-aimer a dressing down, because he had got into the aircraft with muddy boots!

Microfilm of original drawing of Mod 464 provisioning

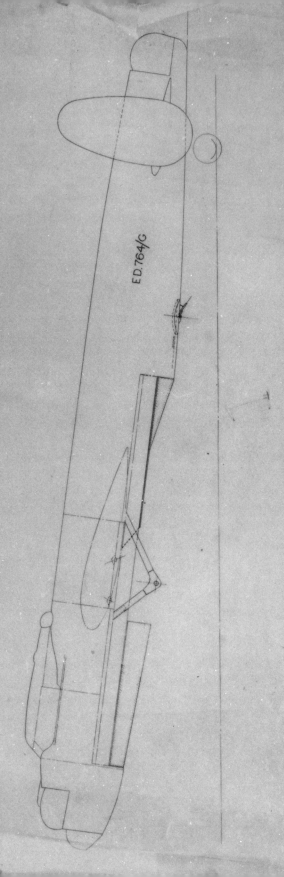

ED.764/G

THE INFORMATION CONTAINED IN THIS DRAWING IS TAKEN FROM Z.2752.

THE GAP BETWEEN SIDE ARMS = 5'-0"

A. V. ROE & Co LTD   AERONAUTICAL ENGINEERS,
MANCHESTER & LONDON.

ISSUED BY:-

— TITLE —

SPECIAL LANCASTER

TYPE

AVRO
LANCASTER

DWG Nº

AVRO LANCAS

SHOWING 464 PROV

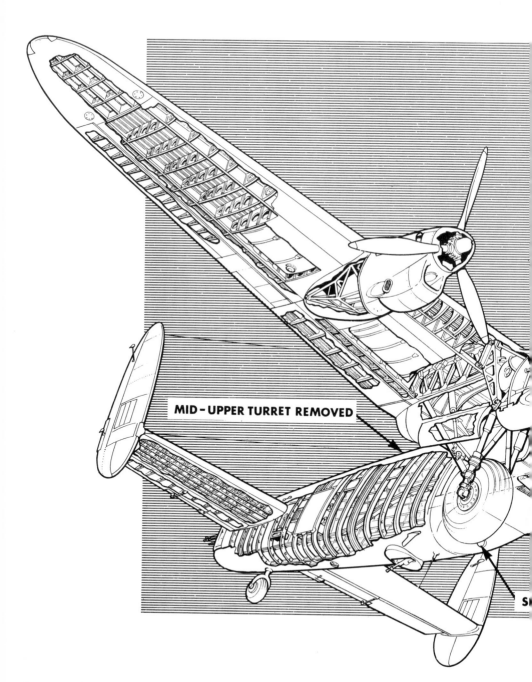

MID-UPPER TURRET REMOVED

Cutaway of Lancaster BIII Special

B III SPECIAL
NG INCORPORATED

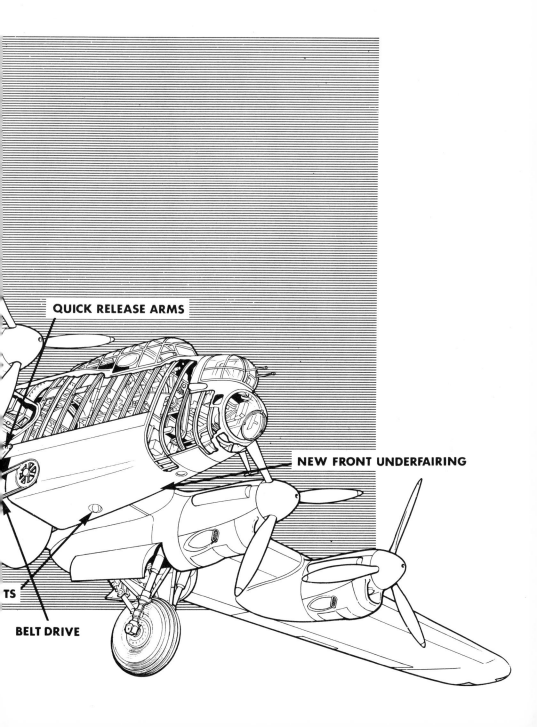

QUICK RELEASE ARMS

NEW FRONT UNDERFAIRING

TS

BELT DRIVE

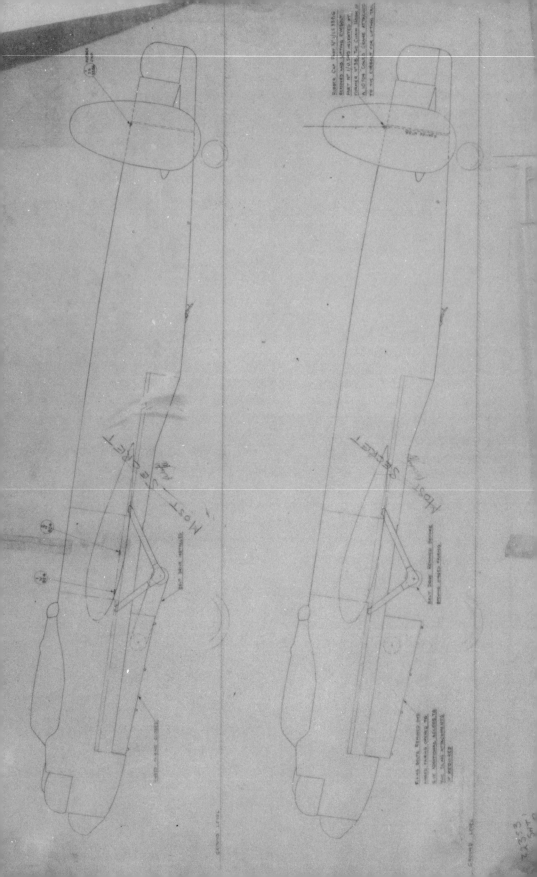

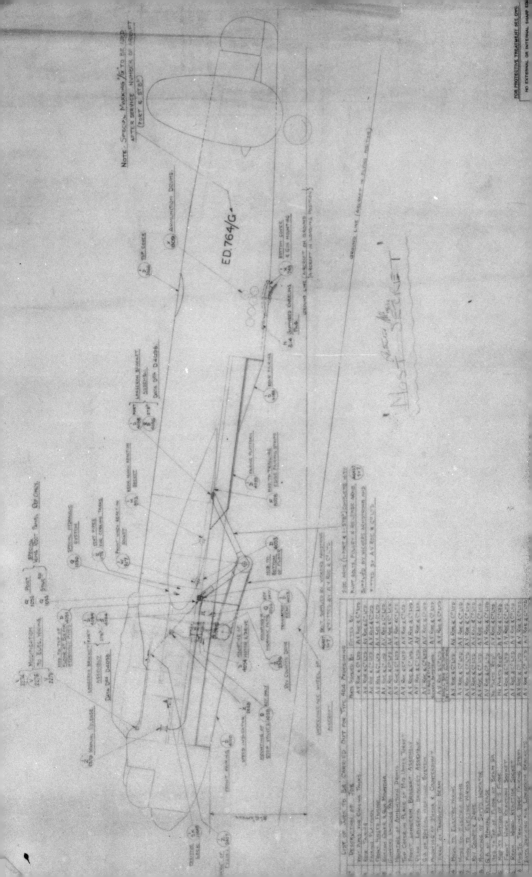

Early one morning, a long convoy of lorries entered the base, heading for the armament dump. They were the new bombs arriving and 'Doc' Watson, the armament officer was there to greet them. The bombs were still warm to touch, having been freshly filled with explosive just before the lorries had left. The armourers handled them with great care.

The squadron had been training now for nearly two months, and they still did not know what the target was. Many had made good guesses but there was still much speculation. Now that the weapons and new aircraft had arrived, everyone felt it would not be long before the mission itself. They were quite right, but there was still more training ahead of them.

On the morning of May 6th, the final training conference was held in Gibson's office. All crew captains were there, seated around the office in easy chairs. Also present were Capable Capel and Doc Watson. Gibson was seated on the windowsill, with Nigger curled up in Guy's chair keeping an ever watchful eye on the visitors. Guy explained that over the past few weeks they had been training individually for the raid, and now the time had come for them to simulate the raid itself. The initial problems had now been solved, he told them. All that remained now was for them to do a practice attack so that an operational plan could be worked out for the actual mission. They had reached high standards during their individual training; now he wanted to co-ordinate them as a team.

Arrangements had been made by the SASO with the property department of a film company, to build a mock-up of their target on the reservoirs at Uppingham and Colchester. The aircrews in Guys flight who would attack the Moehne and Eder dams would attack singly. Gibson would lead the first attack. He impressed on everyone the necessity for keeping the height and speed correct. This time they would be using the real weapon, the bouncing bomb. The charges would be the same as used on the actual mission, so once the bomb had been released they were to get clear in a hurry.

Other crews not on this mock raid would continue practising height and speed runs over the Wash. Their turn would come next, for these were the crews who would attack the Sorpe dam.

Gibson then asked if anyone had any suggestions? Dinghy Young had. At the moment, the front gunners feet dangled in the face of the bomb-aimer. Could something be done to provide foot rests for him? This would not only be more comfortable for the gunner in his front turret, but the bomb-aimer would not be worried about having his head bashed continually by a pair of flying boots.

Someone else suggested fixing a second altimeter at eye level with the pilot. Nigger snored away contentedly in Guy's chair while his master listened to the flood of ideas. Those he approved involved enough work to keep the ground crews busy for the next few days — when they could get into the aircraft.

Gibson had drawn up a list of code words for use on the raid. These were peculiar to this one mission, and this one squadron. 'Nigger' stood for the destruction of the Moehne dam, 'Dinghy' for the Eder, and there were many others. Each of the captains was told to get a copy and memorise them.

They broke up the conference, leaving Nigger in a blissful sleep.

The next week a full dress rehearsal of the raid was held with senior officers in attendance. But it was a fiasco from start to finish, due to faulty intercommunication. This was cured by fitting VHF fighter voice radios into the Lancasters and throwing out the morse-keys. The next rehearsal was a complete success. Voice radio procedure was alien to bomber crews. Radio sets had been fixed up in the crew room, and the whole squadron did radio drill until they became competent at it. Mock raids were carried out in the crew room, until everyone got the hang of it.

There was not much time now. Photographs conveyed the news that the dams were nearly full. The whole squadron was trained and bursting to go. When would they get the green light?

The Operation

On 15th May, the AOC came to see Gibson. He brought the news that 617 wanted to hear. Practice was over. In twenty-four hours it would be the real thing. After a few words to Guy, wishing him and the squadron good luck, the AOC left. As soon as he had gone, a little white aircraft flew in and taxied round to the

GUY GIBSON'S LANCASTER

Length o.a.	69ft.6in.
Wing span	102ft.0in.
Height (tail up)	20ft.6in.
Wheel track	23ft.9in.

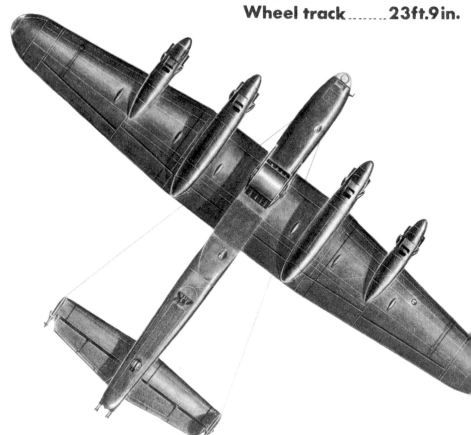

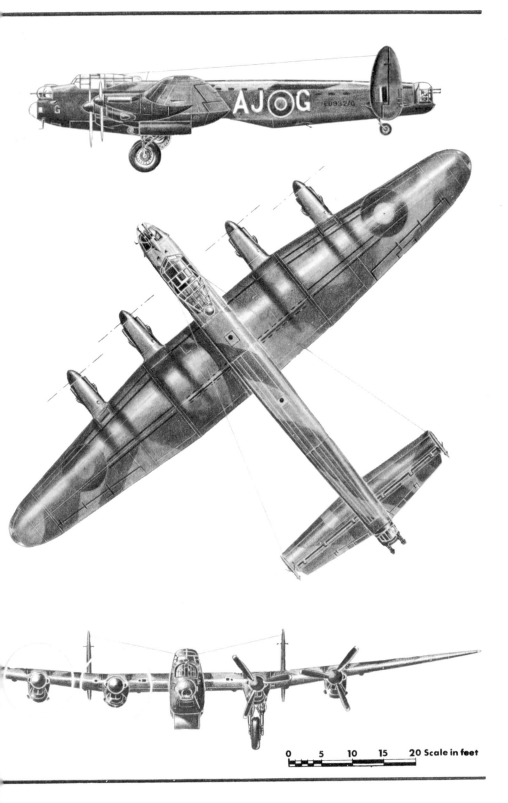

0   5   10   15   20 Scale in feet

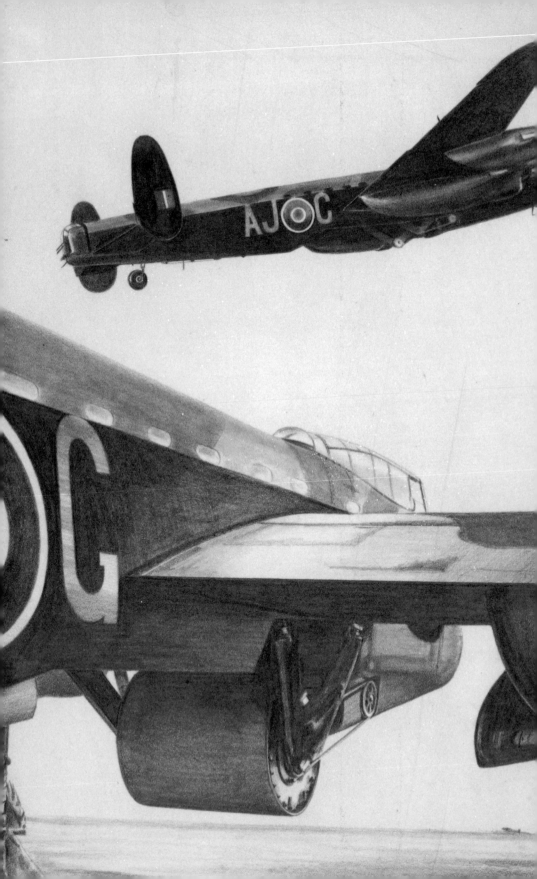

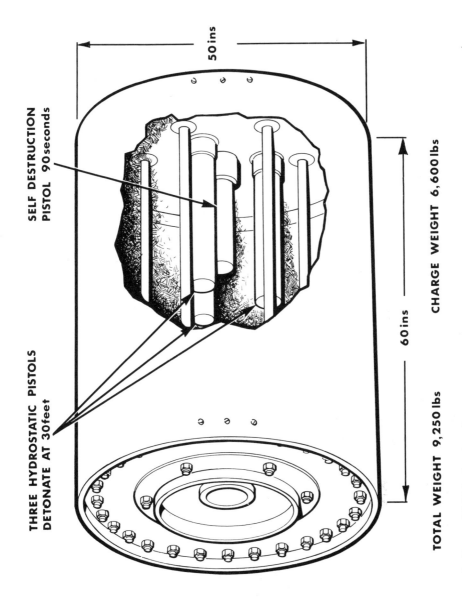

SELF DESTRUCTION
PISTOL 90 seconds

THREE HYDROSTATIC PISTOLS
DETONATE AT 30 feet

50 ins

60 ins

CHARGE WEIGHT 6,600 lbs

TOTAL WEIGHT 9,250 lbs

Dr Barnes Wallis's dam-busting weapon

Left
'C' for Charlie and Guy Gibson's aircraft —
two of the 'Scampton Steamrollers'

MISSION FORMATION

FIRST WAVE

'P'
F/L MARTIN

'G'
W/C GIBSON

'M'
F/L HOPGOOD

'A'
S/L YOUNG

'Z'
S/L MAUDSLAY

'L'
F/L SHANNON

'J'
F/L MALTBY

'N'
P/O KNIGHT

'B'
F/L ASTE

SECOND WAVE

'T'
F/L McCARTHY

'H'
P/O RICE

'K'
Sgt BYERS

'E'
F/L BARLOW

'W'
F/L MUNRO

THIRD WAVE

'C'
P/O OTTLEY

'O'
F/Sgt TOWNSEND

'S'
P/O BURPEE

'Y'
F/Sgt ANDERSON

'F'
F/Sgt BROWN

big black 617 hangar. Out of it stepped Wallis and Mutt Summers. Now that all the final preparations were in hand, they wanted to be with the Squadron and help in whatever way they could.

Gibson sent for his flight commanders and their deputies. When they were in his office he told them their targets. They discussed the planned routes that he and the SASO had worked out to evade the enemy flak positions. The squadron were to be glad of that little conference, because the planned route in fact would have led them over new enemy gun positions that Pickard had not known about. It was Hopgood who told Guy about these guns, guarding a big rubber factory on the edge of the Ruhr. At midnight the meeting broke up and everyone headed for bed. Guy was just about to leave the office himself, when Charles Whitworth burst in with the sad news that Nigger, who had gone for a walk, had just been run over by a car outside the main gates of the station. He had died instantly. This was a bitter blow to Guy, who loved his dog. Anyone who owns a dog will understand his feelings at the news. He took it to be an omen also, and asked if Charles would keep it to himself. No use upsetting the rest of the Squadron. Next day he had a few words with Chiefy Powell about Nigger's funeral, asking him to keep it quiet. He wanted the dog buried at midnight that night, when he would be over the target.

That morning the whole base was amazed to hear over the Tannoy public address system the call for 'All crews of 617 Squadron to report to the briefing room immediately'. The other squadron on the base had been 'taking the micky' out of 617 for quite some time now, even to the extent of writing a sarcastic song about them. This was the first time the crews of 617 had been summoned to the briefing room, so the whole base was agog with excited speculation. Could it be that they were actually going to go on ops?

When Gibson entered the crowded briefing room with Wallis and Mutt, the chatter stopped. One hundred and thirty-three young pairs of eyes followed them from the door to the platform at the end of the room. When Gibson had seated his two visitors, he turned to the assembly. They were a tired, scruffy-looking bunch, but the look of expectancy on their faces once again made him remember his own early days in that very same room.

He introduced Wallis to the gathering, and left it to him to tell them the target. When Wallis told them, in his quiet manner, what it was all about, Guy noticed the look of relief that came over their faces. He knew from the recce photos that security on the base had been good, for otherwise the Germans would have increased their defences of the dams. They had not done so. Wallis explained everything to them, much as he had done to Guy — how the bomb worked, why this date had been chosen for the mission, why they must not expect the first bomb to blow a hole in the dam's wall. When he had finished the atmosphere was one of relief. This job was not half as bad as they had expected.

For the ground crews, the rest of the day was going to be one mad panic, but for those at this briefing, it was going to be a day of studying maps and putting in final air tests on the aircraft to make sure that everything was in tip-top shape for the raid that night. Later, after lunch, the three crates that Gibson had helped to unscrew in the AOCs office were brought into the briefing room. For three hours the crews studied them, until they knew every gun emplacement, every tower and tree.

Later in the afternoon, just before tea, a final briefing was held. Once again the loudspeakers blared out calling all 617 Squadron aircrews to report to the briefing room. This time when the boys came trooping over to the briefing room they found two service policemen at the door, and each man was asked for his identity card and checked off on a list. No unauthorised person was allowed in the room. As soon as everyone was gathered within, the doors were locked. The security for this raid had been well kept.

Once again Gibson faced the meeting. Behind him on the platform were Wallis, Cochrane and Whitworth. Gibson started by telling them this was the final briefing before the raid. In a little while they would be taking-off to do the job for which they had been training hard for the past two months. He then made way for Wallis, who told them more or less the same things he had said earlier that day, this time adding a bit more to his lecture by telling them of some of the difficulties he had run into in the development of the weapon.

Next to speak was the AOC, who gave them his own brand of pep talk. Cochrane was a good speaker, and could hold an audience without the need for notes. One of the things he told them was that they were going on a mission that would go down in history. When they got back after the raid, they would be famous. Many people would ask them how they had done it, what sort of bomb they had used, and many other things. They were questions which must remain unanswered. The weapon was on the secret list and other plans were being drawn up for its use. He wished them the best of luck on their mission and said that he knew they would succeed.

Gibson spoke again. He kept them for an hour, explaining the flight plan and the kind of attack they would use. There were two types of attacking methods being used during the raid. One they knew well enough, the technique used on the Moehne and Eder dams. The other was the method to be used against the earth dams like the Sorpe. Gibson had divided the squadron into three main groups for the raid, the first group consisting of himself, Hopgood, Martin, Young, Astell, Maltby, Maudsley, Knight and Shannon, and their crews: this group would attack the Moehne and Eder dams.

The second group consisted of McCarthy's, Byens', Barlow's, Rice's and Munro's crews. They would attack the Sorpe, the Lister and the Ennepe dams. Because these dams had to be attacked with a different technique, the training these crews had been undergoing was altogether different from that of the first group. If anything it was more dangerous, because in their case they had to attack across the width, not the length, of the dam, also no spin was required in dropping their bombs. Their object was to place their bombs on top of the dam's parapet.

Lastly, the third group, consisting of the crews of Townsend, Anderson, Brown, Ottley and Burpec would be the standby group. They would travel with the second wave, but should they be required to fill any gaps in the first group, they would do so. They had been busy learning both types of attacks, just in case an emergency arose and the first group never made their target.

Then the meeting broke up, each man was left with his own private thoughts. Gibson had wished them all 'Good Luck' saying there would be 'a hell of a party tomorrow night' and the drinks would be on him. With that, the service police unlocked the door.

The crews trooped out into the cool evening air and headed for the Mess. When they returned, they were in flying kit, to wait by their aircraft for take-off. Not much was said, for the intensive training they had been going through had been a strain on their nerves, the more so because they had not known the target. Now they knew where they were going. The mission was upon them.

Gibson himself was very run down. A carbuncle had developed on his face, making the wearing of an oxygen mask most painful. He had worked harder than anyone, with the sole exception of Wallis.

Now the crews on McCarthy's flight were climbing into their machines, for it was time for them to depart. From somewhere a red Verey light streaked upwards into the night sky. That was the signal to start engines, and almost instantaneously 36 engines burst into life. Engines were tested, instruments checked out, and a host of other jobs on the pre-flight checks were done. Then it was time to assemble at the end of the runway for take-off.

Slowly, from their dispersal points, the great black machines trundled round the peri track, heading for the end of the runway. There they waited for a signal from the control caravan, granting them permission to take-off. McCarthy's flight would be first away, leaving ten minutes before Gibson's. There were two approach routes to the Ruhr, chosen as a safety factor so that the Germans, plotting their courses in their underground operations rooms, should not guess their targets. The route that McCarthy would travel to the Sorpe was longer than the one Gibson would take to the Moehne. As both groups were due to attack their respective dams at the same time, the Sorpe party left first.

The first three aircraft took up their positions for take-off. A green light flashed from the control caravan. Opening up their engines to full throttle, the pilots released their brakes and the machines surged forward. As the controls came to life in their hands, the pilots raised the tails off the runway. The aircraft were now eating up the runway, taking a longer run than usual to be free. At last they were airborne, climbing steadily into the evening sky, to circle, waiting for the rest of the flight to join them. Soon they were all away, heading out over the Wash towards the enemy coast.

Guy Gibson and crew

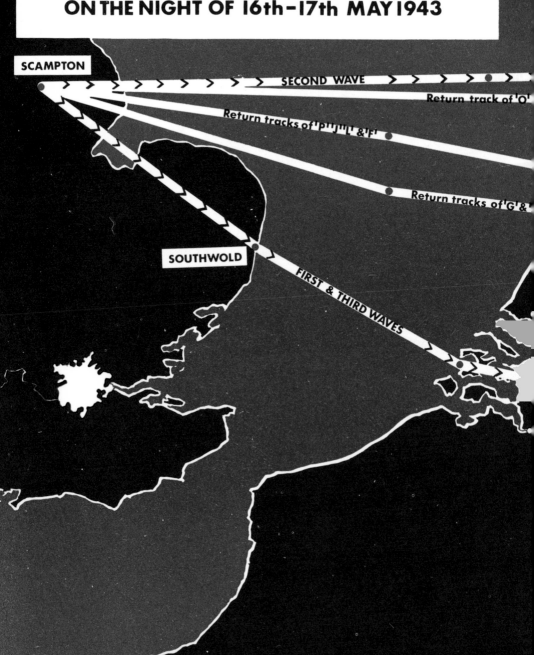

'W' Flt. Lieut. Munro
returns to Base

'H' Pilot Officer Rice
returns to Base

'E' Flt. Lieut. Barlow
'K' Sgt. Byers
Missing in this section

'A' Sqdn. Leader Young
Lost here on return

'M' Flt. Lieut. Hopgood
Lost during attack

t Officer Burpee
ere

DORTMUND

MOHNE DAM

'B' Flt. Lieut. Astell
Lost here

ENNEPE DAM

SORPE DAM

EDER DAM

COLOGNE

LISTER DAM
(Not Attacked)

'Z' Sqdn. Leader Maudslay
Lost during attack

A few minutes later it was Gibson's turn. Again at a signal all the engines burst into life. Then they also were taxying round for take-off, to await the green light. Then it came once again, and the night air was filled with the mighty roar of Merlins. In a few minutes they too had gone, leaving the countryside peaceful once again. It was a lovely evening, with a full moon. 617 Squadron was the only squadron operational this night. The moon was too bright for the mainstream boys.

As the noise of their engines faded into the distance, those remaining settled down to the interminable waiting. The ground crews retired to try and snatch a few hours sleep. Until their aircraft and crews came back there wasn't much they could do.

Wallis and the AOC both went to the control tower, to await any radio messages that might arrive. The aerodrome was now a very quiet place. The moon bathed the place in a light bright enough to read a newspaper in. Everywhere was quiet.

Both flights were to keep complete radio silence until they had crossed the enemy coast. On that flight across the sea, as each crew settled down to his job, many of them must have wondered if they would make it back.

Below them the moon was bouncing off the top of the waves. They kept down low, flying at about 60 feet. The crew of a minesweeper were surprised to receive a message from one of the last aircraft in the formation. It had been flashed at them with an Aldis lamp, and read: 'We're going to get drunk tomorrow night'. They waved in return, but did not know what what these mad 'Brylcream Boys' meant.

The two flights were making steady progress on their separate routes across the North Sea, McCarthy's flight taking the more northerly course. So far everything had gone well. Over the Zuider the first disaster struck when P/O Rice misjudged his height over the smooth flat water. He touched the water with his bomb, doing a speed of over 250 knots. There was a terrific jolt as though some giant hand had swiped at the weapon. So severe was the shattering blow, that not only did it knock the weapon off but the two outer engines tore themselves out of their mountings! But in spite of this the great Lancaster staggered on, and by dint of sheer good airmanship, Rice managed to get the aircraft up off the water to a height of a few hundred feet. His companions saw his plight but had to press on. There was nothing they could do except to flash a signal telling him to get back to base. As soon as he had taken stock of the situation, he turned back. The officer on duty in the control tower heard the lone aircraft circling an hour later. He eventually spotted the strange machine circling Scampton, but didn't recognise the aircraft. In the moonlight it looked more like a Whitley than a Lancaster, but he flashed his green Aldis giving permission to land.

Later, when Rice and his crew had a good look at the aircraft, they realised how lucky they had been. But thanks to a good skipper, they had made it. Then another aircraft circled, wanting to land. This was Flight Lieutenant Munroe's aircraft. He had been so badly damaged by flak over Holland, that he had been forced to abort the mission. Again the skill of the pilot was clearly indicated by his safe arrival and landing, for he came back with his bomb still on board.

This now left only three aircraft in McCarthy's flight. They still pressed on, now skirting Stavoren and Harderwijk, then disaster struck again. First, Flight Lieutenant Barlow was hit by flak. What happened to him is not clear, but his aircraft ploughed into the ground and there was an almighty flash as his bomb went off. After the explosion, all that remained of his aircraft were a few smouldering pieces of wreckage, flung far and wide over the countryside. Flight Sergeant Byers and his crew must have suffered the same fate, for nothing was ever seen or heard of them again. This was the fate of McCarthy's flight: he pressed on alone, seeking the large black lake that was his target. The standby flight following McCarthy had been divided up to attack three separate targets. Pilot Officer Burpee, Pilot Officer Brown and Flight Sergeant Anderson would also attack the Sorpe, but Pilot Officer Ottley and Flight Sergeant Townsend were to attack the Lister and Ennerpe dams respectively.

Below, in their underground bunkers, the Luftwaffe controllers had been patiently plotting the progress of 617 Squadron. Their task was twofold, firstly to pre-warn towns in the paths of the oncoming British planes, and secondly to direct the night-fighters in to attack. So far, it had not been easy to get a definite fix on the British aircraft, for their low altitude was making it difficult. Neither were the controllers sure of the target that was to be attacked. It looked as though two separate groups of bombers were coming in to attack some of the heavy industrial towns in the Ruhr. Suddenly, however, the British planes headed towards the Ruhr Mountains, away from the big prize of the Krupp empire.

When McCarthy reached the Sorpe, he circled the hills taking stock of the situation and deciding on his best approach. Luckily he met no opposition in the form of flak or night-fighters. Even so, the task in front of him was difficult. He made eleven runs in before he was finally satisfied he could place his bomb in the correct position. On his twelfth run he released his bomb and it fell dead on target. The following explosion shook the hills round about, and the blast wave made the Lancaster buck and rear like a horse in an American rodeo. Then a column of water and dust rose several hundred feet into the air, hanging there for what seemed hours to McCarthy. Not until it had drifted away could he see the result of his attack. He discovered his bomb had scored a direct hit, but had not breached the dam. Feeling disappointed he turned for home, if only the others of his flight had made it! There was always the hope that some of the reserve flight had got through and would be able to come in and finish the job. Wallis had been right. More than one bomb would be needed to do the job on the earth dams.

The next crew to arrive was that of Pilot Officer Brown. He came after McCarthy had departed. Again, after a circuit of the dam, he noticed the damage caused by the first attack. To place his bomb in the same position as McCarthy's would be difficult, but he had to try. Once again it took twelve attempts, but finally the bomb landed squarely in position, and the hills shook once more under the explosion of one of Wallis' specials. After the dust and spray had cleared, Brown saw there was a breach in the dam. It wasn't much of a hole, but the next man in must surely finish it off. Brown turned thankfully for home.

Anderson was the next to arrive. He found the lake peaceful, but with a heavy mist settling in the valley. He could not locate the wall of the dam and the mist hid the damage caused by his predecessors. After making several attempts, he eventually gave up, returning home with his bomb.

Burpee and his crew never made it. Nobody knows what happened to them.

By this time Pilot Officer Ottley had nearly reached the Lister dam. What happened to him however, is a complete mystery; he was never heard of or seen again. Flight Sergeant Townsend on the other hand made a good attack on the Ennerpe, but failed to breach it. This mist was becoming too thick now, and dawn was starting to show its first light over to the east.

Gibson, who had taken off ten minutes after McCarthy's flight was luckier on his run in to the target. They crossed the Dutch Islands, weaving in and out of the known flak positions. Crossing Holland without mishap, they were now flying over Germany, having passed Eindhoven on their starboard side.

They headed for the Ruhr via the Rhine to Duisburg. Flying along the Rhine, they encountered some opposition from barges fitted with light flak guns, but the rear gunners of the aircraft gave as good as they got. Only thirty minutes away from the targets now. Passing on into the Ruhr Valley, they met some more light flak, but by weaving the aircraft about and keeping low, they avoided heavy damage. Many a time they were picked up in the beam of a searchlight, before they dodged behind clumps of trees.

Once they passed over a brand-new well defended airfield not marked on their maps. A running battle ensued with the flak guns, the rear gunners aiming at the searchlights. Flight Lieutenant Astell, momentarily blinded by the beam of one, lost control of his aircraft. The great machine reared up, stalled and crashed into the earth, its weapon exploding with an enormous flash and a tremendous bang. Then darkness swallowed the shattered Lancaster.

The first wave flew on, passing Dortmund and Hamm. Then came the sight they were all looking for, the Ruhr Hills. A few seconds later they saw the dam itself, looking very forbidding indeed, the water smooth as glass with the moonlight reflecting off it. It was an awesome sight, but this was no time to admire the view, for the defences around the dam had opened up on them.

Balls of green, yellow and red came streaking up at them.

Gibson circled the dam, picking location points, getting ready for his run in. A final check over the radio to the rest of the first wave found them all present, with the exception of Astell. Warning them to stand by for their attacks, he started his run in. Circling the great lake, he went up to the far end, and with the moon behind him came in low over the water towards the dam. On came the two spotlights, down went the aircraft until the two beams formed a figure eight, speed a constant 232 mph. The bomb aimer in the nose was taking aim with the crude homemade bombsight, having set into motion the equipment that made tbe big bomb revolve on its special racks.

The flak started again as they approached, the nose-gunner in the aircraft answering. Flak was coming up thick and heavy now. It was a pure freak of fate that it did no damage, for Gibson's aircraft could not vary off course once he had started his bomb run.

Then the bomb-aimer called 'Bomb gone', the aircraft gave a great leap and a few seconds later was clear of the dam, and out of range of the flak guns. The rear-gunner gave them the news of the explosion over the intercom, and when Gibson turned in again to circle the dam, he could see a great column of white spray at least a thousand feet high. It took ten minutes for the great lake to calm down once again, enough for the second aircraft to start his run in.

By this time the enemy knew what the targets of the special squadron were, and Gibson himself admitted later that their tracking and warning system was first-class. He was not surprised to find plenty of enemy night fighters hovering around the dam. However, the great Lancasters were flying too low for them to attack, so they had to be content to sit and watch the raid, hoping to attack as the 617 boys returned home.

Now it was the turn of Flight Lieutenant Hopgood and his crew in 'M-for-Mother', for Gibson's bomb, although exploding at exactly the right spot, had not breached the dam.

Hopgood commenced his run in, his spotlights came on and down he went to the correct height above the water. He was making a good run in, when suddenly he was hit by flak, for now

Construction (top) Destruction (bottom) of the Moehne Dam

the gun crews knew what to expect and from which direction the attack would come. The aircraft was hit in one of the inboard fuel tanks and flames started to appear, then a long fiery jet streamed behind the aircraft. The bomb aimer must have been hit, for when the weapon was released it went over the dam, landing on the powerhouse below. Meanwhile 'M-for-Mother', was trying desperately to make height so that some of the crew could bale out. Hopgood reached about 500 feet, when there was a terrific explosion and one of the wings came off. The aircraft hurtled to the ground and could be seen by the remainder to be burning in a field about three miles past the dam. Then there was a blinding flash as the weapon that Hopgood had released went off on the powerhouse. A great pall of smoke arose and took about fifteen or twenty minutes to clear.

The next crew to run in was Flight Lieutenant Martin's, and this time Gibson went in with him. The two aircraft raced across the top of the water, guns blazing, as they came in range of the flak. Martin's bomb-aimer did a good job in placing the bomb, while Gibson's gunners tried hard to take care of the flak gun crews. Once again they flew over the dam wall and into safety beyond, and once again the water churned up from the great underwater explosion, as the bomb exploded behind them. There again was the great lake writhing, with a great column of water rising as before.

Both Martin and Gibson were safe, although Martin's aircraft had been hit and lost all the fuel from one of his tanks. Luckily there was no fire.

Next crew in was Squadron Leader Young's. Gibson gave him a warning about the flak. In came 'D-for-Dog' from the far end of the dam, lights on and down to height. In came Gibson again, attacking the flak defences, running in with Young's aircraft, but at a safe distance. Again the water erupted as the bomb exploded in the correct position, but still the dam held!

It was Flight Lieutenant Maltby's attack next, and by this time the tension in the crews was getting high. Would the dam *never* go? In came Maltby, lights on, down to height, steady at 232 mph. Target in sights, bomb gone.

This time it *must* go!

The Moehne Dam the morning after the raid

Once again the water churned up under the explosion of the bomb, once again up came the great column of white spray. It was difficult to see now, for the air seemed to be full of a misty spray that covered their windscreens. Gibson, who had placed himself in a better position to see that explosion, thought there seemed to be an awful lot of water going over the top of the dam. This may have been an illusion. From where he was, it was difficult to tell properly. Flight Lieutenant Shannon was the next one in, but Gibson ordered him not to make his run until he had had a closer look. His investigation revealed a gap of about a hundred yards across, with water gushing out and into the valley below. The whole face of the dam wall had toppled forward down into the valley, carried there by the force of water. Wallis's shock wave theory was proved correct.

The flak gunners had retreated to safety with the exception of one brave man, who still kept to his post, firing at Gibson as he came in to see the results of the raid. He did not survive the Lancaster's gunners for long.

Gibson's radio operator sent out the word 'Nigger' so that those back at base should know of their success, although back in the Ops room at Scampton, they had been listening to the R/T conversations of the crews for quite a while. Barnes Wallis was amongst the crowded Ops Room staff, well pleased with the results of the raid so far, as were the other VIPs.

For a while the crews of 617 at the Moehne watched the water racing down the valley, sweeping everything before it. They could see the headlights of cars, speeding along before the great tidal wave and then being overtaken by it, their lights vanishing under the water.

Instructing Maltby and Martin to return home, Gibson called the remaining crews to follow him to the Eder dam. They set off, again flying at tree-top height, along the valleys of the Ruhr Hills and reached the Eder Lake. Gibson was first there, and called the other crews to check in on the R/T. They sounded rather faint and it was obvious to him that they were slightly off course, so he told them he would fire a red Verey light over the lake. This he did, and soon he was joined by the rest of his flight.

The Eder dam was to prove the skill of the pilots, for unlike the

Moehne Lake, which was long and without bends, the Eder was of a snaking formation, having much steeper walls to the surrounding hills. It meant coming in at 1000 feet and dropping smartly down to 60 feet, levelling out, releasing the bomb and making a quick turning ascent to avoid a mountain facing the dam.

Time was running out. Over to the east the faint light of dawn was appearing, and these Lancasters were not built for daylight battles.

The first one in on this attack was Flight Lieutenant Shannon, but it was an aborted run. Somehow he could not manage it and after five attempts reluctantly contacted Gibson and asked permission to withdraw for the time being. He would not release his weapon until he was sure he was on target.

Gibson called in 'Z-for-Zebra' next, Squadron Leader Maudslay's aircraft. After two runs, Maudslay gave the following crews some advice on how best to tackle this most difficult run in, then said that he was going in on his final run. They saw his aircraft drop down and his lights came on, then they knew he was at the correct height. He was flying straight and true. The watching aircraft saw him release his bomb, but too late. It struck the top of the parapet and exploded on impact. They saw the great Lancaster hurled upwards in the brilliant flash from the bomb, a flash that lit up the whole valley. Nothing was ever seen or heard of Maudslay or his crew again.

A great pall of smoke hung about over the parapet of the dam. There was no point in attacking while the target was obscured, so the remaining crews flew about until it was clear.

Then it was Shannon's turn again; after one dummy run he seemed satisfied, and he went for a perfect run up to the dam wall. He placed his weapon just in the correct place, then he was over the top of the parapet, climbing steeply, almost vertically, and away. The weapon went off and the waters beneath them were seething, then they burst and the great column of white spray they had seen so many times at the Moehne dam, came up to greet them.

The time spent waiting for the atmosphere to clear seemed endless and the light in the east was getting brighter. Now it was clear again and Pilot Officer Knight's turn. Once again it was not

until the third attempt that he was satisfied. Gibson saw his weapon bouncing along the top of the water, strike the parapet and sink slowly to the bottom. This was the last bomb left, so Gibson kept his fingers crossed that this would be the one to breach the Eder. They watched anxiously, then saw the explosion hurl great chunks of masonary from the face of the dam, as though a giant hand had punched a hole in it. Then the water was gushing out through the hole and into the valley below, a great tidal wave again, heading for Kassel.

The time had come to send the code word 'Dinghy' and head for home. On the way they followed the rushing splashing torrents of the Eder, watching as it swept away everything in its path. Power stations became submerged, and the electrical supply for the whole area was wiped out. Ahead was one of the main and most modern training airfields of the Luftwaffe, with underground hangars and sleeping quarters, soon to be submerged.

Their course for home took them over the Moehne valley, and below they could see the devastation that they had caused only a short while before.

The rear-gunner on Gibson's machine had fired nearly 12,000 rounds of ammunition during this raid, so far.

It was now quite light and, as the great machines headed for home, they still kept close to the ground. One aircraft (it was never discovered which of the missing crews it was) went a little too near Hamm and was attacked by night fighters and shot down. Then came Duisburg, with fires still burning from an attack the night before by other squadrons. It would not be long before the water from the Moehne reached the town and put the fires out. On went the remaining aircraft, hugging the ground like great black eagles. The enemy was groping for them, but the light conditions were such that the 617 crews had the advantage. Because of their camouflage and low altitude they were difficult to detect from above, and they were flying too low for enemy fighters to get underneath them. But they were not out of the wood yet, Gibson's navigator told him they would be out of Germany in fifteen minutes, those minutes went by like hours. However, Rotterdam eventually appeared on their port wing tip,

The Eder Dam the morning after the attack

then once again they were speeding over the waters of the North Sea.

Back in the Operations room at Scampton, Wallis was overjoyed. His three years of hard work had paid off, the mission was a success.

Air Chief Marshal Sir Arthur Harris congratulated Wallis and Cochrane, and insisted on telling Sir Charles Portal, Chief of the Air Staff, who was in Washington at the time, of the success of the mission.

Of the eighteen aircraft taking part in the mission, eight did not return, and of these eight crews there were only two survivors, who were taken prisoners. Fifty four men perished.

It was a tribute to those who died, that the squadron was kept alive, for more operations were being planned, and a squadron crest was in the making. Guy Gibson's name has become legendary, as has that of his famous dog 'Nigger'.

The formation of a special squadron (617) had, it was realised, given the RAF a unit that could deal with other problem missions. This story describes only one, but the squadron history is a glowing one. The 617 Squadron motto is '*APRES MOI LE DELUGE*'. It might well have been 'We succeed where others fail.'

Thirty three decorations were awarded to the aircrews of 617, most of whom already had several to their names.

Gibson was awarded the Victoria Cross.

The other awards were:
DSO —
  Flt. Lt. Joseph Charles McCarthy, DFC, RCAF;
  Flt. Lt. David John Harfield Maltby, DFC, RAFVR;
  Act. Flt. Lt. Harold Brownlow Martin, DFC, RAFVR;
  Act. Flt. Lt. David John Shannon, DFC, RAAF;
  P/O. Leslie Gordon Knight, RAAF
Bar to DFC —
  Act. Flt. Lt. Robert Claude Hay, DFC, RAAF;
  Act. Flt. Lt. Robert Edward Hutchinson, DFC, RAFVR;
  Act. Flt. Lt. Jack Frederick Leggo, DFC, RAAF;
  F/O Damel Revil Walker, DFC, RCAF

Gibson's crew at de-briefing after the Dams raid

DFC —

 Act. Flt. Lt. Richard Dacre Trevor-Roper, DFM;
 F/O.s Jack Buckley, RAFVR;
  Leonard Chambers RNZAF;
  Harold Sydney Hobday, RAFVR;
  Edward Cuthbert Johnson, RAFVR;
 P/O.s George Andrew Deering, RCAF;
  John Fort;
  Cecil Lancelot Howard, RAAF;
  Frederick Michael Spafford, DFM, RAAF;
  Harlo Torgar Taerum, RCAF

Conspicuous Gallantry Medal (Flying) —

 Flt. Sgt. Kenneth William Brown, RCAF;
 Flt. Sgt. William Clifford Townsend, DFM

Bar to Distinguished Flying Medal —

 Sgt. Charles Ernest Franklin, DFM

Distinguished Flying Medal —

 Flt. Sgts. George Alexander Chalmers; Donald Arthur Maclean, RCAF; Thomas Drayton Simpson, RAAF; Leonard Joseph Sumpter; Sgts. Dudley Percy Heal; George Leonard Johnson; Vivian Nicholson; Stefan Oancia, RCAF; John Pulford; Edward Webb; Raymond Wilkinson.

On May 27th 1943, the King and Queen came to visit the squadron. They congratulated everyone concerned personally, and chose the squadron badge and motto.

Guy Gibson

Many thousands of men and women were in the armed forces during the last world war, and many performed heroic deeds. It befell only a few to be what we could call today, the 'Superstars' of valour — Guy Gibson was one of them. For his heroic leading of 617 Squadron on the Ruhr dams raid, he was awarded the Victoria Cross, the highest award Britain can offer a member of her serving forces in time of war. But this was not his only decoration, for he also had the Distinguished Service Order and bar, and the Distinguished Flying Cross.

He was born in 1918 at Simla in India. His father was serving as

Guy Gibson

Conservator of Forests there, but later was transferred back to Britain, settling in Kent where Guy grew up. When he was old enough Guy went to St. Edwards School in Oxford. Keen on all sports, he developed a very athletic figure, although he never did grow much in height over five feet, although he always had boundless energy.

Gibson became interested in flying as a career late in his teens. His first thought was to become a test pilot, but as with most young lads of those days, he did not realise the education required for this job. He soon found out when he applied for a job with Vickers Armstrong at Weybridge. The person he saw on his interview was Mutt Summers, with whom he became firm friends in later years. On this occasion however, Mutt was to disappoint him. Companies in the Aircraft Industry do not usually train their test pilots, but prefer to recruit ex-service pilots for the job. Guy of course was not to know this. Mutt gave him some sound advice when he told him that his best plan would be to join the RAF and get plenty of flying hours in before he came back for a job as Test Pilot.

Guy took his advice and enrolled in the RAF for pilot training. He found, however, that here again things went wrong for him. He was told he was too short! It must have been a bitter blow to him and no doubt any lesser person would have given up there and then, but not Guy. He was determined to fly. After many weeks of exercising and stretching, he again applied and this time was accepted. They say that 'where there is a will, there is a way'.

Always with that job at Vickers in mind, he became a serious student at Cranwell. The training period for a pilot in the RAF seems almost endless, but Guy revelled in it. It soon became obvious to his instructors that he would not only become a good pilot, but a wise leader also, for he had not only the personality, but the flair to lead.

He was destined never to achieve his goal as a Test Pilot, for the political situation was to keep him in the RAF. At the outbreak of war, he was flying a Hampden in No.83 Squadron which was based at Scampton, later to become his home base when he started the famous 617 Squadron. At this time, however, it was the period of the 'Phoney War', when nothing seemed to be happening. All the

King George VI choosing 617 Sqdrn's crest, with the motto 'After us the deluge'

action at the time was centred in Europe, and people in Britain began to wonder if they would ever see any action. There were those even who wanted to see what war was like, others who hoped they never would.

The job of the RAF in those early days was to strike at targets in enemy-held Europe. Later when the British and Allied soldiers were driven out of Europe by the enemy, via Dunkirk, the role of the RAF changed. Fighter Command was to become a defensive force, while Bomber Command was the only striking force left to Britain and her Allies. During this period, Gibson found himself on raids in his Hampden, over occupied Countries, sometimes even minelaying in the North Sea. During the Battle of Britain, he took part in strikes against invasion barges which the enemy was collecting across the Channel.

It was the policy of the RAF to send aircrew who had served what was known as a 'tour of operations', into units not considered front line, for what they wisely called 'rest periods'. Gibson had the choice of going on a rest period, or being transferred to Fighter Command. He chose the latter and was sent to No.29 (F) Squadron stationed at Digbey, a night fighter squadron equipped with Beaufighters. He quite enjoyed his time with this unit, and succeeded in shooting down three enemy aircraft. So much for a 'rest period'.

With any service, one must take the rough with the smooth, but it was a bitter disappointment to Guy to find himself posted to an Operational Training Unit — OTU — He was the type who liked to get to grips with the enemy. Nevertheless this posting had its good points for him. He did manage to get a bit of home life for he had married a lovely young actress named Evelyn Mary Moore while stationed with 29 Squadron. The role of a flying instructor was not for Gibson, and it soon became obvious to his new bride that Guy was longing for action again. How to get back into it was the problem. Gibson wrote for an interview with the new C-in-C of Bomber Command — Arthur Harris, and it was granted. Two days after the interview, he received a telegram telling him to report for duty as the new commanding officer of 106 Squadron, stationed in the North of England. With the posting came promotion to rank of Wing Commander. The squadron, equipped with Manchesters,

H.M. King George VI talks to Flt.Lt. Joseph C McCarthy of Brooklyn

was shortly to be re-equipped with Lancasters. Guy was glad to be back on operations again, and he soon found the squadron to be a happy one. Under his leadership, it became one of the better squadrons in Bomber Command, and it was this very factor, with others, that Harris took into account in selecting him to lead and command the Dams raid.

After this great raid Guy was forbidden to fly further operations. Once again a deep depression settled over this little terrier of a man. Churchill was asked to take him on a tour of America, due in a few days. The Dams raid had caught the imagination of the free world, and Gibson had no option but to go when asked by the Prime Minister.

On his return from America, Gibson thought seriously about starting a political career. This was not for him. He found the ways and by-ways of politics too devious, to say the least; he found that something more than sincerity and wisdom was required to be a politician. So he elected to stay in the RAF, after turning down offers of directorships in industry.

Again he could not settle down to a desk job, which simply went against his nature, so once more he volunteered for operations. This time however it was not so easy for him but after badgering his superiors, he eventually got a posting. It was while acting as master bomber on a raid carried out by No.5 Group on Reydt, that he was killed on his way back home after the raid. He crashed the Mosquito aircraft he was piloting into a hillside, some sixty miles from the target. The Dutch buried him. But, to this day, nobody is sure how he came to crash. His name will always be remembered in connection with the raid on the Ruhr Dams. Bomber Command had just cause to be proud of him, and the Squadron he formed is still operational to-day, maintaining the same high standards he set.

Mr T.O.M. Sopwith presents Wing Cdr. Gibson a model of the 'Lanc' at the Dam Busters Dinner

OPERATION JERICHO

OPERATION JERICHO

And it shall come to pass, that when they make a long
blast with the ram's horn, and when ye hear the sound
of the trumpet, all the people shall shout with a great
shout; and the wall of the city shall fall down flat, and
the people shall ascend up every man straight before
him.

(Joshua 6:5)

Overture

The winter of 1943-1944 was a long and bitter one. In northern
France, still under German occupation, the population watched
and waited. Convinced that the Allied invasion of Europe must
soon come, they were impatient for the signal to rise and bring
their fight for freedom out into the open.

In the Somme province, the people of the wide, flat plains of
Picardy, despite the oppressive restrictions imposed upon them by
their German invaders, gave encouragement and support to their
local Resistance fighters. The Maquis groups in this area were both
numerous and active. They supplied a steady stream of information regarding the latest German military movements to Allied
intelligence headquarters in London, and were responsible for
preparing and maintaining local escape routes for Allied airmen
and escaping prisoners-of-war. In addition to their espionage
activities they were well skilled in the art of sabotage, their recent
train wrecking operations with the resultant deaths of hundreds of
troops had especially caused the German authorities much
concern.

In response to the growing menace that these groups presented,
the Germans and the Vichy Police intensified their investigations
and arrests. Those unfortunate enough to be caught were
summarily tried and sentenced to deportment as slave labour,
internment in a concentration camp — or to death.

Towards the end of 1943, Resistance networks in the Somme
province suffered a severe setback. By seven o'clock on the
morning of the 13th November most of the members of the

Amiens OCM (*Organisation Civile et Militaire*), except for a few who had managed to escape had been arrested. They had been betrayed by a traitor in their midst, introduced in the guise of a visiting member from the Paris OCM. In less than a fortnight the secret army had lost many of its most competent men.

One of the arrested men was Dr. Antonin Mans, Public Health Officer and Head of Passive Defence for the Somme District. He was taken to Amiens prison and put in a cell on the second floor. On the following day he was taken out and interrogated, but his captors, despite their suspicions, learned nothing of his affiliations with the Amiens Resistance movement. As a responsible member of the organisation Dr. Mans knew that every effort had to be made to warn those of his colleagues still at liberty of the traitor within their ranks. With so many under arrest there was always the additional risk that Gestapo interrogation methods might expose what remained of the seriously damaged circuits. After much thought he hit upon a plan that might solve the problem. Because of his medical position, he was allowed a visit from his secretary to whom he dictated a completely fictional report on a local outbreak of diptheria. In this he was able to insert a warning message couched in medical terms to be passed to the Resistance.

But for many it was too late. Despite this clever ruse, the Gestapo continued their relentless persecution campaign and the arrests mounted. December came, and with it many grim tragedies were enacted inside the high walls of Amiens prison. During this month twelve members of the French Resistance group known as the FTPF (*Francs-Tireurs et Partisans Français*) from the Mers-les-Bains sector were executed by firing squad. Other members — like twenty-year-old Jean Beaurin, a skilled saboteur responsible for the derailment of a number of troop trains en route for the Eastern front — lay in their cells awaiting a similar fate.

One of the main French Resistance organisations working under the direct control of the British intelligence service was known as the 'Sosies'. It was led by the Ponchardier brothers, Dominique and Pierre. Dominique's area of command covered the whole of northern Occupied France, whilst Pierre's covered southern France below the demarcation line.

Dominique Ponchardier, an alert determined man, was also a

resourceful and fervent patriot. Endowed with the ability to
organise and lead his fellow countrymen in their dangerous
profession, he knew better than most how ruthless and relentless
would be the German effort to destroy the networks. The Amiens
resistance forces were divided into two separate classifications:
intelligence groups and action groups. Each group normally
comprised a team of about six, and although they worked in
co-operation with each other, all groups received their orders
independently and directly from one leader. Deeply concerned for
the fate of those imprisoned in Amiens jail, Dominique conferred
with his colleagues in an attempt to try and find some way of
releasing them. Desperate measures were obviously called for, or
the so called, 'political' prisoners would shortly either be executed
or deported.

Despite the fact that the despicable practice of shooting
hostages and reprisal prisoners picked at random from the local
populace was frequently carried out by the German occupation
authorities following a Maquis action, it was decided that an
armed raid on the prison by Resistance forces would be the
quickest and best course of action. Such an undertaking would, of
course, depend on careful planning, and it was to further their
arrangements that a second meeting was called. To make and keep
an appointment in public was at this time particularly dangerous,
proof of the Gestapo's increased vigilance. The rendezvous chosen
was a cafe behind Amiens railway station. Ponchardier's assistant,
Pépé, was to meet two other comrades, Maurice Hollville a leading
FTPF member and another Resistance agent named Serge. Then
disaster struck. Minutes before the meeting took place the Gestapo
searched the café and Serge was arrested. Hollville escaped and
forewarned Pépé just in time. Ironically enough, shortly after the
incident Hollville was himself arrested over a comparatively trivial
business of receiving stolen ration cards, and followed Serge to the
cells at Amiens prison.

These new and unexpected developments forced Ponchardier to
re-appraise the situation. Serge was known to have had on him
part of a map of Amiens prison just prior to his arrest. Assuming,
therefore that they had found it, the Germans might well be
prepared for just such an operation as he had planned. As if to

reinforce any last doubts that he might have about the feasibility of the projected operation, Ponchardier received news of a similar armed raid carried out by the FTPF in the Aisne sector against the prison at St. Quentin. An attempt to release prisoners there had resulted in complete failure.

By January 1944, many more arrests had followed the abortive St. Quentin operation, and anticipating further trouble the Germans had tightened up security arrangements at all prisons.

After the café incident, Pépé had been forced to go into hiding, but later rejoined Ponchardier when the latter called another conference. Ponchardier's sea-faring deputy, Revière, completed the trio. The object of the meeting was to consider an alternative course of action. Together they reviewed the facts. January had certainly been a black month for the Resistance forces. True, much good work was being done by those who remained, but their ranks were thinning. Amiens prison now held 700 prisoners, men and women, of whom approximately half were 'political' prisoners. Moreover, word had been received that another batch of executions was imminent. To remain inactive was unthinkable — and yet what could they do? It was Ponchardier who first mentioned the RAF. At first the others did not fully comprehend his line of reasoning. As if thinking aloud he explained: a low level bombing attack with the breaching of the outer walls as the primary object. If the guard's quarters could be bombed and some of the guards neutralized, so much the better. Perhaps a combined operation? The Maquis standing by ready to dash in through the breached walls once the planes had departed.

That his plan was not immediately received with enthusiasm was understandable. Ponchardier himself had realised the consequences should the RAF bombs fall wide of their targets. The prison was full of people. Inevitably there would be casualties, though to what extent it would be impossible to predict. They paused to ponder this matter before resuming discussions. These unknown factors *must* be put aside. Their first duty lay in engineering the release of their colleagues. Anxieties gradually receded as they began to discuss the proposed operation in greater detail.

At last they dispersed, more confident now that they had a

Dominique Ponchardier

positive plan. First, Ponchardier must contact London to ask for the help of the RAF. But here Ponchardier decided to be devious. The direct type of approach for this type of operation, coming as it did at a time when the Allied air forces were so heavily committed to the destruction of the German war industry and many other priority targets, might produce a curt refusal. Instead, he began to filter to London through normal channels, detailed information relating to Amiens prison; the lay-out, construction, defences, guard positions, even details of the anti-aircraft defences around Amiens itself. All this was passed on, along with the location of German Panzer units in the vicinity of Amiens.

If Allied intelligence was puzzled by this rather specialised information it received, it said nothing. After due examination, it was filed for future reference. Meanwhile, Ponchardier continued his struggle to keep the 'Sosies' operational as best he could.

Early in February, the Germans dealt the network a double blow. M. Raymond Vivant, *sous-préfet* of Abbeville and a key Resistance figure, was arrested by the Gestapo. His responsibility for the Coastal sector, and his knowledge of German military defences prior to the 'D-Day' landings, made him one of the most important members so far caught. Hidden in his office were a number of secret documents relating to German coastal defence installations. Cleverly concealed amidst his normal business correspondence they were not discovered during the initial Gestapo search that followed, and were later smuggled out to safety by friends. M. Vivant was taken to Amiens prison under escort, searched and put into cell 16 on the ground floor, there to await interrogation.

On the same day the Germans also succeeded in capturing two Allied agents, and they too were taken to the prison. Jubilant Gestapo agents boasted of even more impressive results in the near future.

Ponchardier could delay no longer. He sent a message through to London, a carefully worded appeal for help. He described the efforts of the Germans to destroy the groups, of the many arrests, and the adverse effect that all this was having on Maquis operations in the sector. The resultant decline in morale, he stressed, gave cause for alarm. He and his men wanted tangible proof the Allies were prepared to assist them in their hour of need. Could they, the Allies, not devise and undertake an operation, for instance, to free their colleagues awaiting their fate in Amiens prison? He drew their attention to the fact that details regarding the prison were already in their possession. If they agreed to his proposal, they would have to act with the utmost urgency. It had now been confirmed that 12 men were to be executed in the prison on the 19th or 20th of February, and many more were now under sentence of death. He earnestly implored them to give their most serious consideration to his request.

The message sent, Ponchardier anxiously awaited the reply. As a leader, he carried a heavy burden of responsibility, but despite the doubts and fears in his mind, his faith in his Allied friends remained unquestionably strong.

When Ponchardier's urgent request for help was received by Allied Intelligence in London, it was passed with the minimum of delay to the Air Ministry. The idea however did not generally find favour, and was treated with some scepticism by those in high office. Nevertheless, the appeal continued on its journey along the chain of high command.

Air Chief Marshal Sir Trafford Leigh-Mallory, Commander-in-Chief of the Allied Expeditionary Air Force, studied it before passing it on with his comments to Air Marshal Coningham, Commanding 2nd Tactical Air Force. He in turn decided to consult Air Vice-Marshal Basil Embry, Air Officer Commanding No.2 Group. The Mosquito Wings in his Group were specially trained for low level operations and had built up an impressive record of accurate pin-point attacks on small targets. Embry was sympathetic to the scheme, for he had himself sampled German captivity in 1940 when, as a Group Captain, he had been shot down and taken prisoner during an operation over France. He had escaped from his guards and, with the help of French patriots, had successfully accomplished the hazardous journey through Occupied France back to England.

He now told Coningham that he thought the operation might be practicable but suggested that he be allowed to investigate the matter in greater detail before definitely committing himself. Coningham agreed and Embry immediately began his research.

D2

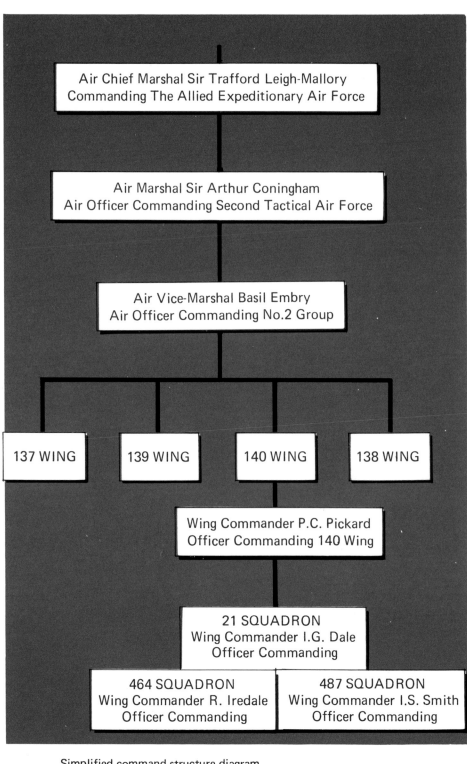

Simplified command structure diagram

His first step was to request that a high-altitude PRU aircraft photograph the area in which Amiens prison was located. When the film had been developed and interpreted, he had No.2 Group's own modelling section construct a scale model of the prison and its immediate surrounds. These models were of great assistance to the aircrew and operational planners in simulating approach conditions when carrying out low-level operations. Next, he obtained, through Intelligence, all the existing information relevant to the prison. Most of this was readily available, thanks to Ponchardier's stratagem and additional details were quickly supplied by the French on request.

Embry's dossier on the prison grew. It now contained the vital information that he required; constructional specifications; internal lay-out; details of the cells, their doors and locks; guard positions and movements, together with prison routine. There were many facets connected with an operation of this nature, and Embry knew that some of these would call for specialist advice. The foremost obstacle to be tackled was the cracking open of the prison itself. Here he decided to call in his pyrotechnic experts and lay the facts before them.

The problem that he presented to them was twofold.

First, what amount of explosive force would be required to breach the thick wall surrounding the prison?

Second, how much explosive would be needed to damage or hole the walls of the prison itself, and at the same time throw the cell doors out of alignment with their locks.

If these problems could be satisfactorily solved, then the right conditions would have been created to favour a mass escape. At the same time there could be no doubt regarding the inherent penalties for this type of action against a prison packed with people. Casualties would be unavoidable among those prisoners in close proximity to the explosions.

Embry felt it his duty to contact the Resistance through London to ensure that they were fully aware of the consequences if the operation was proceeded with. Their reply was short and emphatic. They gave their assurance that the prisoners would rather be killed by the RAF bombs than die at the hands of the

Germans. Even if only a few were saved, they felt that the sacrifice would have been worthwhile.

The acceptance of these calculated odds by the Resistance did little to relieve Embry's already burdened conscience. The ultimate responsibility for the operation, plus the risk of killing our own allies weighed heavily on his mind. Yet despite his personal feelings and the doubts nurtured by some senior officers as to the validity of the operation, Embry held firm to his belief that the object of the mission could be successfully accomplished. Having completed his preliminary investigations he now reported back to Coningham. Official sanction was received, and Embry set the machinery in motion.

The mission, originally known by the code-name Operation 'Renovate' and later changed to Operation 'Jericho' was now definitely on.

The time had now come to choose the men and the weapons for the mission. Having been so actively involved in the preparations it seemed natural to Embry that he should lead the air operation himself. Under his leadership 2 Group were fast gaining recognition for their daring low-altitude operations, and the professional ability of the aircrews had already reached a high standard. Embry experienced first-hand knowledge of this ability when, as often as he was able, he flew missions incognito with the Squadrons as 'Wing Commander Smith'.

Operational improvements which had so far been achieved had largely revolved around the successful introduction of a new aircraft — the de Havilland Mosquito.

Here at last was a high-performance aircraft capable of delivering bombs with great accuracy at low level. With its new Mosquitos 2 Group was now working to perfect a new technique which was to be used many times on small targets in the forthcoming months.

At the beginning of 1944, six Mosquito squadrons were operational in 2 Group, and had been giving an excellent account of themselves against V-1 Flying Bomb launching sites. They had already flown nearly 700 sorties against the sites, which were difficult targets, well camouflaged and heavily defended — despite which Mosquito losses had been proportionately light.

Three of these Mosquito squadrons, 487 (New Zealand), 21 (British) and 464 (Australian), together formed 140 Wing. It was this Wing that Embry chose to carry out the attack. His decision was greatly influenced by the number of veteran crews in the Wing skilled in the tactics and bombing techniques required for this type of operation.

On the afternoon of February 8th Embry flew to Hunsdon, Hertfordshire, home base of 140 Wing since December 1943, the main purpose of his visit being to brief the man who was to be his deputy leader, the Officer Commanding 140 Wing and a man of outstanding ability, Group Captain P.C. Pickard, DSO, DFC.

Twenty-eight year-old Percy Charles Pickard, universally known as 'Pick', was already something of a legendary figure, and ranked as one of the most experienced bomber pilots in the RAF. Born in Handsworth, Sheffield, this sixteen stone, fair haired Yorkshire giant had joined the RAF in 1937 on a Short Service commission.

A number of postings during 1938-1939 enabled Pickard to gain flying experience on a variety of aircraft, but his debut in aerial warfare did not take place until early in 1940. Flying Wellington bombers he took part in the frantic operations against the Germans during the Norwegian campaign. The possessor of a wry sense of humour, Pickard would recount the time when, on returning from one operation, he was forced to ditch his damaged aircraft in the North Sea. He and his crew spent fourteen hours afloat in a rubber dingy before being rescued. The sea being rough, they shipped a considerable amount of water, and, naturally, as he had the biggest feet, *his* shoes were used for baling out!

Pickard continued to fly a steadily increasing number of missions over enemy occupied territory, from France and the Channel invasion ports, to the heavy industries of the flak-infested Ruhr valley in Germany itself. In July 1940 he was rested from operations and in recognition of his services awarded the DFC and promoted to flight lieutenant. The 'rest' was short-lived; almost immediately he was instructed to assist in forming a night bomber squadron composed entirely of Czechoslovakian airmen who had escaped to England early in the war. Although beset by a multitude of problems, an intensive training programme was initiated and in early September the squadron became operational.

Air Vice-Marshal Basil Embry

Pickard continued to fly with the Czechs for the next nine months.

It was about this time that Charles Pickard's face became widely known to the general public. A semi-documentary film entitled *Target for Tonight* was being made by the RAF. Against the background of life in an operational bomber unit the film followed the fortunes of a Wellington bomber, 'F-for-Freddie', and her crew in a night action over enemy territory. The cast were all chosen from members of the RAF, and Pickard was asked to play the role of the aircraft's pilot.

Whatever the film lacked in acting ability, was more than compensated for by its authenticity. For Pickard at least, it was a remarkably true piece of typecasting. The film, acclaimed by the public, captured some of the patriotic fervour of the times, and proved a great success.

Shunning the publicity of the silver screen, Pickard returned to re-enacting his film role in reality. By now a Squadron Leader, he was once again totally immersed in the bomber offensive against Germany. Recognition of his work with the Czech squadron had resulted in the award of a DSO in March 1941, and his exploits over Mannheim brought his name to the attention of the Free Czech Government, who awarded him the Czechoslovakian Military Cross.

In February 1942, Pickard, promoted to Wing Commander and given a squadron of Whitley Bombers, planned, trained and led the air element that dropped British paratroops over the German *Würzburg* radar installation at Bruneval, resulting in the capture of secrets vital to the Allied cause. For his part in this successful venture he was awarded a bar to his DSO.

By now Pickard's experience had made him a man much sought after for other tasks, and this meant several postings during the forthcoming months. Then, in November 1942, he was sent to a special duties unit engaged in landing and retrieving Allied agents from enemy-occupied territories. He flew a miscellany of aircraft — Lysanders, Hudsons and Halifaxes. The work was not without risk, for although the missions were undertaken at night it was often necessary to circle the dropping point or landing zone, chancing interception by enemy night fighters, until ground

Group-Captain P.C. Pickard

contact was made. It was during those secret air liaisons that he made many firm friendships with members of the Resistance. Their scorn and contempt for the enemy coupled with their resourcefulness and determination to strike back won Pickard's admiration. His outstanding work in co-operating with the French while with this unit, earned him a second bar to his DSO.

Nine months later Pickard was promoted to Group Captain and in October 1943 became the first commanding officer of 140 Wing, No.2 Group, 2nd TAF. Although by February 1944 he had completed over 100 missions, he still firmly refused to be grounded, preferring the seat in the cockpit to the chair behind the desk.

Pickard's friendship with members of the French Resistance was well known to Embry. He also knew that if he did not give him the opportunity to help his friends in their hour of need, Pickard might never forgive him.

Thus it was that when the two men met on February 8th and Embry outlined his plan, Pickard's enthusiasm, upon learning that his Wing has been entrusted with the proposed operation, was unbounded. He wanted to 'get cracking' right away to ensure the safety of the prisoners — his friends.

The latest news that Embry had received was that 120 patriots had now been tried and condemned to death. The first batch was to be shot on the morning of the 19th February.

In the light of this information it was decided to launch the attack on the first day of suitable weather after the 10th. Midday had been chosen as being the most appropriate time for the attempt, based on advice passed on by the Resistance. Eighteen Mosquitos were to provide the striking force, with a squadron of Typhoons to act as cover and escort. Embry would lead the first two waves of aircraft, whilst Pickard held a third wave in reserve.

Pickard agreed to select his crews and, as soon as was practicable, withdraw them from scheduled operations. Embry emphasised that security was of paramount importance; if the Germans learned of the impending attack, there was every possibility that they would carry out the executions immediately.

On the 9th, Embry flew to Hertford Bridge to keep an

appointment with Leigh-Mallory who was to inspect another of Embry's Wings, No.137. When he was preparing to leave, Leigh-Mallory drew Embry aside and asked what progress had been made on Operation 'Jericho'. Embry explained the arrangements made so far in some detail. When he had finished, Leigh-Mallory enquired who was to lead the operation and Embry replied that he himself would do so. Leigh-Mallory made no reply to this, which Embry interpreted as a form of assent.

That same evening, however, Embry received a phone call frc.n Coningham. What the Air Marshal had to say came as something of shock. Coningham had been instructed by Leigh-Mallory to inform Embry that in no circumstances was he to fly on this operation. Embry tried remonstrating with Coningham, insisting that the briefing had been carried out, and preparations were well in hanu to mount the operation almost immediately. Although this was a slight evasion of the true facts -- Pickard being the only person so far briefed — Embry was extremely reluctant to adopt the role of spectator and not share in the responsibility of putting the plan into action. But his protests were to no avail; Coningham was sympathetic but firm. Those were Leigh-Mallory's orders, and Embry would be well advised simply to accept them.

There was now nothing for it but for Embry to notify Pickard of the latest turn of events, and place him in full command of the attack.

The best laid plans contain at least one unpredictable element, and in the case of 'Jericho' that element was a natural one — the weather. Good visibility was essential for the task in hand and although a number of sorties were still being flown, the general weather situation was rapidly deteriorating. The succeeding days brought dense cloud that spread quickly across England and Europe bringing with it intermittent sleet and snow showers. Postponement seemed inevitable.

On the 14th of February, a message was despatched to Ponchardier over the clandestine radio network. It relayed details of the mission as planned, and warned him to be in a state of readiness at midday on any day after the 15th. But to the consternation of everyone concerned, the weather grew worse. On both sides of the Channel, anxious eyes tried to pierce the thickly

D.H. Mosquito Mk.VI of 140 Wing

falling snow that whipped across the Continent, looking for a break that did not come.

Although the weather cancelled all air operations on the 16th and 17th, personnel at Hunsdon were confined to camp on standby. Pickard fretted and grew restless with the delay and inactivity. To a friend and colleague, Colonel Livry-Level — a Free French aviator, known in the RAF as Squadron Leader Livry, who flew as a navigator with 21 Squadron, he confided that he was worried about the safety of their friends confined in Amiens. The situation grew daily more urgent. Somehow they must be freed.

The Mission

Dawn on the 18th found the countryside of East Anglia muffled under a white blanket of snow. Heavy clouds shut out the sun and a ground mist hung over the airfield at Hunsdon adding to the general gloom. The Meteorological office reports for south-eastern England were frankly pessimistic. No let-up in the snowstorms was expected during the day.

For Embry and Pickard it was a day of decision. Despite the adverse weather conditions they could afford to delay no longer; it was now or never. At 08.00 hours the eighteen crews selected by Pickard assembled in the operations room for the briefing. As they filed in, RAF Military Police flanking the entrance checked their identities. Their ranks were joined by an additional crew, that of the Film Production Unit's Mosquito, which would accompany them on the mission. Speculation among the crews as to the target grew. The extra security arrangements suggested that it must be something out of the ordinary. On a table inside the room stood a box, its lid sealed, defying all attempts by the more inquisitive to establish its content.

The stamping of cold feet and hum of conversation died suddenly as Charles Pickard entered the room and walked to the table. A few moments later the crews came to attention again as Embry strode in and stood with Pickard. The Air Vice-Marshal opened the proceedings on a cautionary note. He asked that each man assembled there remember that, should weather conditions prevent the operation from taking place, it must nevertheless continue to be regarded as top secret.

The seals of the box were now broken and the contents carefully lifted out and displayed on the table. Built on a wooden base about four feet square was the replica of Amiens prison ordered by Embry. It was a functional model devoid of superfluous detail and designed to show the target as it might appear to the crew of an aircraft at a height of about 500 feet and at a distance of 4 miles.

Signalling the crews to gather round the table in order to get a better view, Pickard commenced the briefing by explaining what the target was, and why they were going to attack it. The atmosphere in the room grew tense as he told of the imminent execution of over a hundred Frenchmen, and of hundreds more in the cells awaiting the verdict as to their fate. Some, who were about to die, would do so for helping Allied airmen like themselves to hide or escape. To mount a conventional rescue attempt from outside would prove futile and costly; the place was too strongly guarded. He went on to relate how, in a last desperate effort to free their imprisoned compatriots, the French Resistance had conceived the 'jail break' idea and had asked for the help of the RAF in implementing it. Pickard sensed their eagerness to hear how the attack was to be carried out, and the part that they were to play in it. Pointer in hand, he drew their attention back to the model on display before them, and proceeded to describe its various features.

The prison was situated north east of Amiens in flat open fields, some distance from the town itself and alongside the Route Nationale 29, the *Route d'Albert*, a long straight road running east-west and connecting Amiens with Albert, some 29 kilometres away.

The three storey prison building was roughly cruciform in lay-out. The longer arms of the cross ran parallel to the road, one end containing all prisoners taken by the French police, the other end all the women prisoners. At either end of this arm, low, corregated roofed, extensions had been built on to house the German guards.

The shorter arm of the cross ran north-south, and at right angles to the road. The slightly longer, or 'northern' part of this arm contained the men they were to try and help escape, the so called

Diagram showing layout of prison

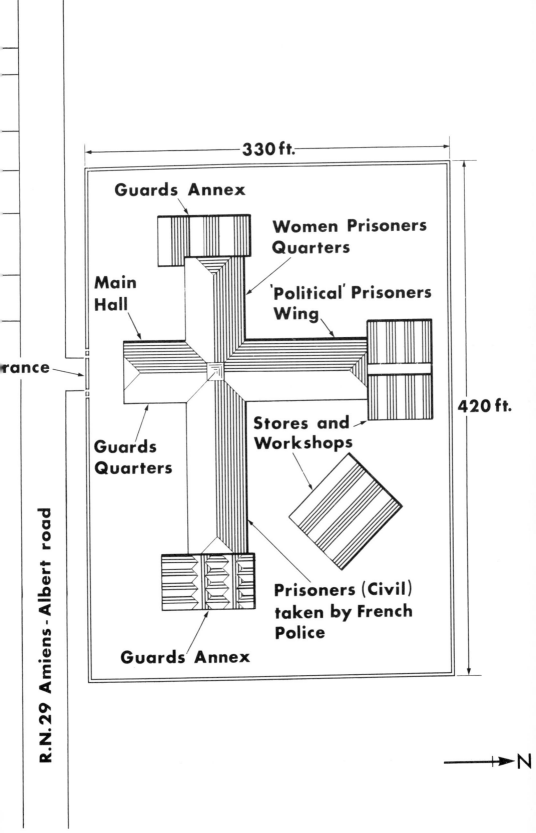

330 ft.

Guards Annex

Women Prisoners Quarters

Main Hall

'Political' Prisoners Wing

rance

Guards Quarters

420 ft.

Stores and Workshops

R.N.29 Amiens - Albert road

Prisoners (Civil) taken by French Police

Guards Annex

N

'political' prisoners. At the inner section of the 'southern' part was situated the main hall, with guards' quarters at the outer end adjacent to the main entrance. At the intersection of the cross, some 60 feet above the ground and built into the gabled roof, was a watch tower manned by German guards, affording them an almost uninterrupted view over the prison and its surrounds.

The compound on which the prison stood was rectangular in shape, and contained various other buildings, workshops, stores, etc. The whole area was surrounded by a high brick wall approximately 20 ft high and 3 ft thick, its top bristling with broken glass.

Pickard paused just long enough to allow his audience time to assimilate the layout of the prison before continuing, they were to be given the opportunity to study the model more thoroughly at the end of the briefing. The group of men standing before him represented all three Squadrons in the Wing. Six crews had been selected from each squadron to fly the eighteen plane-strong 'jail break strike force'. In addition to this force, 198 Squadron were putting up an escort of twelve Typhoons, a ratio of four to each wave of six Mosquitos. The only non-combatant, the Film Production Unit's Mosquito, would formate on the second wave. Take-off was fixed for 11 o'clock, 2 Group operational planning staff had provided the routing both to and from the target area, and their ETA at Amiens would be 12.00 noon. According to information received on the prison routine, the majority of the German guards took their lunch then, so vigilance at that hour was likely to be relaxed. Outside the prison the streets in and around Amiens were normally busy at this hour. If all went well, those who managed to escape would have a better chance of avoiding recapture by mingling with the crowds.

Precise navigation and a fast, low approach to the target would achieve the desired element of surprise at the same time denying the German defences the chance of dispersing the formations. On arrival at the target area, the first wave of six aircraft were to split into two sections of three. The first section using the main road, the *Route d'Albert*, for an accurate final approach to the prison, would bomb and breach the eastern wall. The second breaking away to starboard some four miles from the target would create a

The model of Amiens prison used for the briefing

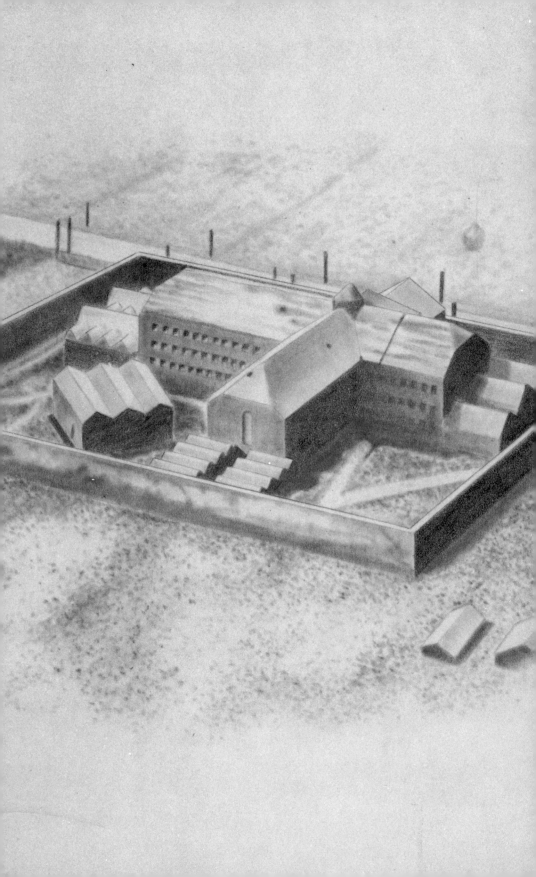

diversion along the railway at Amiens before turning on a southerly course in order to run in and bomb the northern outer wall. By breaching the outer wall in at least two places it was hoped to foil any attempt by the Germans to seal off one of the escape routes.

Pickard carefully emphasised his next words. To minimise the risk of their bombs overshooting the wall into the prison building beyond, their point of release would have to be below the level of the wall, around fifteen feet, or lower. They would then have to pull up immediately in order to clear the 60-foot building on the other side.

Ninety seconds later, the second wave of six aircraft dividing as before in two sections of three, would attack the main prison building itself. Theirs was a task more difficult even than the first wave, for they had to place their bombs precisely at the base of the prison walls. The resultant explosions, calculated to make the cell door locks ineffective, would also blast an exit to allow prisoners a way of escape into the yard and thence through the breached outer wall.

By actually placing their bombs in the low extension buildings at either end of the east-west arm of the prison, it was hoped that the second part of their objective would also be accomplished: that of wiping out the guards' quarters and their occupants.

Here Pickard made a vital point. The success of the whole show would depend on strict adherence to an exact timetable — particularly on the bombing runs. Successive waves of aircraft attacking the target at right angles called for fine judgement on the part of the pilots in order to avoid a mid-air collision. Additionally, as they would be dropping bombs with an eleven-seconds delayed-action fuse, an error in timing could prove fatal for the following aircraft.

Scanning the faces in front of him, Pickard singled out those of the Film Production Unit's crew. They were to run in next, he told them, allowing a sufficient interval for the second wave's bombs to explode, before filming the bombing results.

The third and last wave of aircraft would circle the target perimeter well clear of the attacking force. Held in a reserve capacity, they would be called upon to duplicate the bombing pattern only if the results of the first two waves' attack proved unsuccessful.

Pickard announced that he would make his own bombing run as the last aircraft in the second wave. He then planned to circle the prison to observe and assess the damage. The decision whether or not to commit the third wave would rest with him. The code words 'Green, green, green' over the R/T would bring them in to attack. 'Red, red, red' would signify that the job had been done, and that they were to set course for home immediately.

Should any mishap occur to Pickard's aircraft there would be one other pilot flying across the target at this time who could make an evaluation of the attack and send the signal. This was Flight Lieutenant Tony Wickham piloting the film aircraft. It was arranged for him to act on Pickard's behalf in an emergency.

From where he stood, Air Vice Marshal Embry was able to pay close attention to the proceedings and observe the reactions of the men. He sensed a feeling of elation running through the crews which was not like a normal briefing. They had been given not only the opportunity to save life, unique indeed in their daily routine of destruction, but also the chance to repay the sacrifices made by French patriots in providing shelter and help to their comrades. The keen rivalry that existed between the three squadrons was also manifest when the question of who was to fly the first and second waves arose. Pickard had already earmarked the New Zealanders for the lead, but in view of the special nature of the attack and in fairness to the other two squadrons, he resolved the matter on the spot by tossing a coin. To their undisguised joy the New Zealanders won the toss, the Australians winning second place. The British crews of 21 Squadron, much to their disappointment, were allotted the reserve position.

At this point Pickard concluded the general briefing. The pilots wanted a closer look at the model, to discuss details and to question areas of doubt. The navigators having formed a separate group, gave their attention to the Wing Navigation Officer, Flight Lieutenant J.A. 'Bill' Broadley.

Twenty-three-year-old Broadley, a fellow Yorkshireman, was to be Pickard's navigator on the mission. They had flown on many operations together since they had first met on the bomber base at

Scampton in 1941. The two men became firm friends and respect for each other's professional skill in the air, had resulted in their becoming an almost inseparable team. Postings to different squadrons on occasions over the past four years had forced them to part company temporarily, but in December 1943 they were reunited again when Broadley was posted to 21 Squadron. His courage and ability during his tours of operations had won him the award of the DSO, DFC and DFM, and had often led to opportunities for personal advancement, but he had by-passed these in order to remain with Pickard.

Having seen preparations well under way, Embry decided that he could now take his leave of them. Pickard escorted the Air Vice Marshal to the door, the two men conversing for a moment before Embry left for duties elsewhere.

Around 10 o'clock Pickard contacted No.2 Group headquarters for a final situation check. Met Office reports gave little hope of any real change over England and the Channel, although prospects over the target area were thought to be improving. It was suggested that a short postponement might be advisable. But Pickard felt there was little to be gained by delaying matters further. His main concern was that another postponement could ultimately lead to the cancellation of the entire operation. Time was running out and there was too much at stake.

The crews, on learning of the latest developments, backed his decision unanimously. In spite of the adverse weather conditions they knew they might have to face, they were determined to fly to Amiens that morning.

Out at the dispersal area on the frozen airfield, the ground crews had been working hard to ready the aircraft for flight. Cockpit and engine covers had been removed, whilst wings and tailplanes were swept clear of snow. Refuelling bowsers moved between the aircraft topping up tanks, while armourers and fitters arrived with the tractor-drawn bomb trolleys to bomb-up and rearm, run-up engines and check equipment. Now the activity was over and the Mosquitos stood ready and aggressive, awaiting the arrival of the crews. The briefing room too, was quiet once more now that the crews had departed to prepare for the mission, only Pickard remaining to supervise the removal of the model for security reasons before following the others.

Flight Lieutenant J.A. 'Bill' Broadley

A little before half past ten the crews arrived at dispersal. Running through their own separate checks as quickly as possible they prepared to taxi out. Spluttering into life in the cold morning air, the Rolls-Royce Merlin engines — first starboard, then port — were warmed and left running at 1200 rpm.

One by one, the aircraft taxied out and, turning into line, moved off by squadron along the snow-covered perimeter track. As the close-cowled Merlins had a tendency to overheat during prolonged taxiing, each aircraft moved into its allotted position without delay.

The first six aircraft of 487 Squadron swung off the approach track onto the runway. Behind them, the other two squadrons queued in line astern, ready to follow suit. All aircraft were now in their correct order for take-off which, as briefed, would be at 11.00 hours. The Pilots cut their engines and waited.

Along the line of stationary aircraft, nose entrance doors were opened and pilots and navigators descended lowered extending ladders, glad of an opportunity for a stretch and smoke before setting off. Those who had enjoyed a recent mug of tea with little or no time to spare afterwards were particularly grateful. Urged on by the bitter cold they hurried to the rear of their aircraft in order to 'christen' the tail wheel. Others stamped around their aircraft in an effort to keep warm. Here and there down the line neighbouring crews conversed, pre-mission emotions released in cheerful banter or a joke. Near his own aircraft, *HX 922* 'F-for-Freddie', Pickard stood alone, familiar pipe in mouth, trying unsuccessfully to adjust the straps on his Mae West, until Broadley came to his rescue. As take-off time approached the crews climbed back into their aircraft and sat in the cockpits, counting down the last few minutes, impatient now to be away.

A few minutes before eleven, propellers commenced turning again as the engines of the first Mosquitos were started, sending flurries of snow to the rear. At 11.00 hours permission to take-off was received from Control.

With brakes released and throttles opened as fast as they dared, the first pair of Mosquitos led by Wing Commander I.S. 'Black' Smith, Commanding Officer of the New Zealand Squadron, accelerated down the runway in a spray of fine snow. Succeeding

'O Orange', Mosquito Mk.IV of the Film Production Unit

aircraft took off at intervals of one hundred yards between pairs until all three squadrons were airborne. Circling the airfield they formed up immediately into groups of three, before disappearing from view heading south for Littlehampton where they were to rendezvous with the Typhoons. The film unit's special Mark IV Mosquito was delayed on take-off and made a late start, having to fly flat out to catch up with the others.

The flight south was not without mishap, for soon after leaving Hunsdon they ran into a dense snowstorm. Visibility ahead was reduced to a few yards and crews strained to see through snow bespattered windshields, the wipers hard put to clear an arc of vision. During this period, four Mosquitos, two from 21 Squadron and two from 464, became separated from the main body. Unable to regain contact again, the frustrated pilots were forced to turn about and head for base. The remainder, edging closer together plunged on through the opaque storm.

The Typhoons experienced similar difficulties after taking off from Westhampnett, and only eight aircraft of the projected twelve succeeded in making the rendezvous with the Mosquitos over Littlehampton.

As soon as they set course over the Channel, the now reduced striking force dropped down to within 15 feet or so of the almost flat water. With the Typhoons clinging to the outer aircraft, the Mosquitos closed up their formation. Gradually, some miles from the English coast, they began to emerge into clearer weather.

Fifteen minutes after leaving England they were climbing to 5,000 feet to cross the French coast, near Ver-sur-Mer, 10 miles north-east of Dieppe. Beneath their wings passed the web-like pattern of ice-fringed estuaries and salt marshes of the Somme coastlands.

Despite their reduction in numbers and the appalling weather, so far the flight had gone well. Suddenly, without warning, smoke trailed away from the port Merlin of 'Q-Queenie', a 487 Squadron aircraft in the first wave. The pilot, Flight Lieutenant B.D. Hanaflin, feathered the propeller on the offending engine while maintaining his position in the formation.

After crossing the Dieppe—le Tréport road, the aircraft descended to low level once more and were soon following the contours of the Somme valley. Accelerating and still in close formation, they hugged the snow covered slopes. Cresting the final rise, the flat cultivated plains of Picardy stretched out before them, the vast flat white surface relieved by the fleeting dark contrast of hedgerows and an occasional isolated cluster of farm buildings.

They were within ten miles of the target when it became obvious that 'Q-Queenie's' troubles had not been eliminated. The fire-blackened engine which, in the meantime, Hanaflin had restarted, began to malfunction. With the formation now drawing ahead, Hanaflin decided to jettison his bombs and turn for home. On the return journey the aircraft was hit and damaged by flak. Badly wounded in the neck, Hanaflin continued to fly his aircraft despite the spreading paralysis which completely disabled the right side of his body. He was given morphine injections by his navigator and, although still in pain, with great courage and determination recrossed the Channel making a successful landing at an airfield in Sussex.

The main force had meanwhile swept around to the north of Amiens and headed in the direction of Albert. The formation now broke and separated as briefed. The Mosquitos of 21 Squadron and the eight Typhoons banked sharply away to take up their respective roles of reserve and patrol.

Navigation to the target area had been 'spot-on', for as the first and second waves executed a 90-degree turn, they picked up their target marker, the long, straight grey ribbon stretching across the plains which was the RN.29. On a course that ran parallel with the road, Wing Commander Smith led the first three aircraft of 487 Squadron on their target approach run. The aircraft dropped lower, levelling off at about 15 feet from the ground. Lining the road to their left, black telegraph poles flashed by in quick succession as they leap-frogged hedgerows and trees, the slipstream from their propellers creating a snowy wake behind them. Less than a mile ahead they could see the great dark mass of Amiens prison standing out in relief against the snow. In tight compact formation they throttled back, slowing their aircraft to ensure greater bombing accuracy. At 500 yards they passed the first small cluster of houses on the far side of the road, marking the beginning of the Amiens suburbs.

E

England

HUNSDON ⊚ | 19 MOSQUITOS
TAKE-OFF 11.0 a.m.

LONDON

FORMATION FLIES INTO SNOW
BLIZZARD. 4 MOSQUITOS BECOME
DETACHED AND RETURN TO BASE

WESTHAMPNETT ◎
LITTLEHAMPTON

MOSQUITOS RENDEZVOUS
WITH TYPHOON ESCORT

Belgi

FIGHTER ESCORT OF
12 TYPHOONS TAKE-OFF
FOR LITTLEHAMPTON.
DUE TO ADVERSE WEATHER
CONDITIONS ONLY 8 ARRIVE

ENGINE FIRE FORCES
1 MOSQUITO TO ABORT
MISSION AND RETURN
WHEN ONLY 10 MILES
FROM TARGET

MOSQUITOS ATT
AMIENS PRISON

Le TREPORT

ALBERT

DIEPPE

AMIENS ◎

SOMME   St. QU

France

PARIS

0   10   20 Miles

0   10   20 Kilometres

The outer wall of the prison was now clearly discernible, enabling Smith to pin-point his aiming mark, on the north-east corner. A German patrol that had suddenly appeared, marching around the outside wall, was caught and scattered by fire from the Mosquito's machine guns.

The gap closed rapidly. Endeavouring to place their bombs at the base of the eastern wall, they sank lower still, skimming the ground at 10 feet, less than half the height of their target. The wall seemed to leap to meet them as the navigators pressed their bomb releases, then they were pulling hard upwards and the bombs had gone. With a deafening roar the Mosquitos shot over the prison, throttles opened wide, climbing steeply away.

Despite the efforts made to ensure an accurate delivery, not all the bombs followed their intended course. Tail-fused and falling horizontally, they struck the frozen ground and bounced forward like flat stones thrown at the surface of a pond. One ended up in a field to the north, while others smashed through or over the wall, some careering erratically across the prison courtyard between outbuildings before finally embedding themselves in the west wall — opposite their intended target. The south wing of the prison containing Gestapo offices and German guards' quarters was also hit.

The two remaining 487 Squadron aircraft of the second section that had veered off to the right before the start of the run in, now swung round and approached the prison for their attack on the north wall. The crews of these two aircraft had seen the departure of the first section's Mosquitos after dropping their bombs. Seconds later, a succession of explosions within the prison compound had sent dust and debris flying into the air. By the time they reached their objective the smoke was drifting away at right angles to their line of flight.

With one exception all the bombs of the second section crashed down onto the brickwork of the north wall, breaching it in two places. The single stray bomb overshot, striking the corner of the north wing, the part of the prison building containing the 'Political Prisoners'.

Since, due to bad weather, two of the Australian 464 Squadron aircraft had returned to base, the remaining four in the second

Flight route for the Amiens mission 18-2-44

wave, led by Wing Commander Bob Iredale, had reformed to attack in sections of two. The first section swept in to bomb the German guards' annexe at the eastern end of the prison building. Flying low alongside the road, the Australians aligned their aircraft with the main prison building and, like the New Zealanders, delayed their drop until the last possible moment. The Mosquitos pulled upwards, missing the main building by a few feet. Their bombs overshot the east wall, scoring direct hits on the corrugated annexe roof.

Billowing clouds of smoke had by this time almost totally obscured the western end of the prison when the second Australian section arrived, making the annexe at that end a difficult target to hit. Although it meant almost bombing blind with only the identifiable features memorized from their study of the model to guide them, they adjusted their height and speed and made their run in accordingly. Eleven seconds later the explosions hurled debris from the annexe high into the air.

After the bombing runs Pickard climbed to 500 feet and circled the prison to evaluate the damage. Carefully checking the bombing results against individual objectives he scanned the outer walls first. The west wall had suffered worst. A large section had been demolished at the corner junction with the north wall. The north wall itself appeared to have at least two smaller breaches in it. The east wall, one of their primary objectives, showed small signs of damage here and there, but nowhere along its length was it breached. From the short amount visible under the smoke, the south wall also appeared intact. (Later reconnaissance photographs showed that a breach had in fact been made in the south wall near the main entrance gates).

Inside the pock-marked courtyard, few outbuildings appeared to have escaped undamaged, and it was with some concern that Pickard surveyed the main prison building. Smoke still concealed the total extent of the damage, although it was apparent that the German guards' quarters would need no further attention. The survival chances of their occupants looked very remote indeed.

All this time Pickard had been watching for some signs of life from within the prison, but had seen nothing of the inmates. Anxiety gave way to relief when, seconds later, minute groups of

The first wave attack

figures appeared, scrambling over the debris in the courtyard towards the gaps in the walls.

So, after all the mission had been accomplished.

Aftermath

On the ground below, ten minutes before the attack began, two men had walked up and down in the thick snow along the *Route d'Albert*.

Always keeping the sinister looking prison building within sight, Ponchardier and Revière with another five of their comrades remaining hidden in the background, watched the sky and waited, as they had done each morning since the 16th. The 18th had dawned brighter than the previous two days and local visibility was better. The strain of waiting was beginning to tell on Ponchardier and his men. Briefed and ready, they had been able to do nothing except patrol the surrounding area each day. They could not know of the difficulties encountered by their colleagues on the other side of the Channel. The midday chimes of a nearby church clock reached the waiting men over the white-topped houses and silent fields. Automatically they looked up at the sky again and listened. The echoes of the chimes died away but there was no sign or sound of approaching aircraft. The two men resumed their pacing, each alone with his thoughts.

Since he had received the message from London informing him of their decision to help, Ponchardier had thrown himself wholeheartedly into the task of preparing for the forthcoming operation. He had sought the assistance of the FTPF in the Amiens area. They had conditionally promised lorries and a small army of men after he had sworn on oath that the RAF would not fail them. He had also solicited the help of the occupants of the nearby houses to provide aid and shelter for the escaping men. Other units and even individuals had pledged support with men and transport. Finally, he had smuggled a message into the prison via visiting relatives, warning those whom he knew that he could trust with the secret of the escape plan, to prepare themselves.

He had taken so many people into his confidence in the past few days, to say nothing of the hopes he had raised, that he dared

Amiens prison during attack

not think of the consequences should the escape plan be discovered, or the bitter blow it would be to their cause if the RAF did not come.

Then suddenly they saw them. The aircraft, just black specks against the grey sky at first, circled around Amiens in the direction of the road. Then the formations separated, some breaking in the direction of the railway, while others turned, heading low towards the prison.

Inside the prison, when the church clock had struck twelve the distribution of the midday soup was in progress. Carrying the heavy cauldrons between them, the two-man soup details, accompanied by a guard, slowly made their way from cell to cell. On all three floors the cells were now full, and many of the men and women recently incarcerated within faced an uncertain future. For only the minority of those held charged with petty crimes, was the stay temporary. The 'political prisoners' could entertain little or no hope at all of their eventual release. Even if they were spared the firing squad — the sentence for many of them at recent trials — deportation was the fate awaiting them.

In Cell 16 on the ground floor M. Raymond Vivant, *sous-préfet* of Abbeville, had been contemplating his future at the hands of his captors. Twice interrogated by the Gestapo since his arrest, he now calmly awaited his forthcoming trial and subsequent sentence.

Ponchardier's message, warning of the imminent rescue attempt, had been received by only a handful of people so far, but to the enlightened few it had meant that the prospect of escape was now something more than just a remote possibility. One such recipient of the message was Dr Mans, also confined on the ground floor. The news, smuggled in by devious means, had brought him renewed hope, for like many of his imprisoned colleagues, the recent treachery within their ranks coupled with the suspicions of the Gestapo had resulted in his condemnation to death. Above him, in cells on the first floor, were many others who had been tried and were now awaiting execution. Among them were a few who had received the message, Captain André Tempez, regional Resistance leader, FTPF member Maurice Holleville, arrested after the café incident, and young Jean Beaurin, local FTPF deputy,

After the raid. A reconnaissance photo showing the damage to the north side of the prison

whose mother and brother were also imprisoned there.

At 12.03 the soup detail on this floor had almost reached Cell 27 in which 'Political Prisoner' Marius Couq and his three companions were confined when, with a deafening roar, the first wave of Mosquitos skimmed over the prison roof. Almost simultaneously the wail of air raid sirens from Amiens sounded the alarm. Then the prison vibrated to the crash and thud of the ricochetting unexploded bombs.

As with Marius Couq, the immediate reaction of most prisoners was to climb onto their bunks and peer out through the small cell windows, hoping to catch a glimpse of whatever it was that had shattered the silence. Many believed that an aircraft must have crashed nearby or that an air battle was in progress over the prison. When the bombs exploded they were flung back across the cells, many cut by flying glass or sustaining injuries from their fall. Some of the explosions now seemed to come from inside the prison itself. Shaken by the sudden uproar, men crouched in the corner of their cells or lay on the floor for protection, as explosion after explosion shook the building to its very foundations. Alternate clouds of dense choking dust and great blasts of icy air rushed along the corridors and into the cells, as ceilings, walls, and floors were split by giant cracks and cell doors were dislodged from their frames.

Covered in debris, Marius Couq and his comrades experienced great difficulty in seeing and breathing, due to the great cloud of suffocating dust that had filled their cell. Peering upwards they realized that the ceiling had fallen in, whilst underfoot the floor felt on the point of collapse.

Groping their way across the cell they were eventually able to force an exit through the already damaged door by battering it with a stool. Bloodstained and covered in dirt, they staggered out onto the landing to be confronted with a frightful scene of desolation. The prison had the appearance of having been in the centre of an earthquake. Above them patches of sky showed through the smoke in areas where the roof and sections of the cell blocks on the second floor had collapsed, burying their occupants underneath. On the first floor landing, one or two others were also emerging from their shattered cells, reeling about amid flames, falling masonry and choking clouds of dust. Below them were great heaps of rubble from which, despite the noise about them, they could hear the cries of those trapped and in pain.

By now some prisoners, although stunned and unable to fully comprehend what was happening were beginning to realize that the way for their escape now lay open. Blindly they made their way through the ruins and out into the courtyard with all the speed they could muster. The German guards too had suffered casualties during the attack and were hardly in a strong position to oppose a mass break-out. While some had died at their posts, others had been able to get to their shelters and take cover when the air raid warning sounded. Many were trapped inside their quarters during the extremely accurate bombing of the south wing and the annexes and lay badly wounded or dead. Nevertheless, as the violent explosions ceased, despite the tumult and disorder, bursts of small arms fire rang out, becoming more distinctive as the drone of the aircraft finally receded into the distance. Isolated units of those guards still in command of their faculties were opening fire at random, cutting down the fleeing figures.

Ponchardier and his comrades, forced to delay their entry into the prison until the bombing had stopped, clambered through the nearest breach in the outer wall followed closely by a number of the local inhabitants. On arrival in the courtyard they found that the situation had become extremely confused. German guards venturing out of their shelters now mixed with escaping prisoners in the gloom created by the smoke, making identification practically impossible.

Shaken but otherwise unhurt, M. Raymont Vivant had already made good his escape from the ruins of his ground floor cell. Groping unsteadily through the piles of smoking rubble in the courtyard, he came to a gap torn in the surrounding outer wall. Through it he could see the wide expanse of fields white with snow. At this point, three or four others had arrived, and together they scrambled through the breach, each bent on following his own escape route. M. Vivant set off alone in the direction of Albert.

In Dr. Mans' cell a rapid structural transformation had taken place. The walls were so badly cracked that they seemed about to

collapse, and the blast had literally smashed the door wide open. Through the obscuring dust, Dr. Mans tentatively emerged through the doorway into the main hall and gazed, stunned, at the scene of desolation around him. Looking up, he discovered the roof of the hall was missing and the staircase to the first floor no longer there. Everything suddenly seemed strangely quiet after the noise of the bombing.

One thing only, the desire to escape, had become firmly fixed in his mind. Hindered by falling debris, he made his way through the devastated hall and out into the courtyard. All around him others were fleeing towards the outer wall.

Suddenly, from behind him he heard his name being called. Turning, he looked up and saw Captain Tempez at the window of his first floor cell, shouting to him to be let out. Retracing his steps, he re-entered the building and headed towards the ruined Gestapo offices in the north-east corner of the hall, where, he finally located a key. His next task was to reach the cells on the first floor, for all that remained of the original staircase were the loosely hanging iron supports.

With some difficulty he scaled the supports up onto the first floor landing. Fortunately the key that he had found fitted and he was able to free Tempez, but there were others in cells nearby, shouting to be let out. The key passed from Dr. Mans into the hands of new arrivals on the scene who set about releasing those still imprisoned. Descending by means of the staircase supports once more, Dr. Mans reached the ground, determined to escape while there was still time.

As he retraced his steps into the courtyard, he became conscious of cries of distress and pain around him, as wounded prisoners were being carried or helped out of the prison buildings by their comrades. Almost at once he came upon a woman lying on the ground, her legs severed. A man, obviously deeply distressed, knelt by her side cradling her head, oblivious to the fleeing figures around them.

Dr. Mans suddenly found himself torn between his duty to his country and his duty to humanity. On the one hand, he had been given the opportunity to regain his freedom and fight back, to assist in rebuilding the shattered Resistance networks which, after

Amiens prison after the attack. Inset: Top left Dr Antonin Mans. Bottom right. M. Raymond Vivant

the recent treachery was of paramount importance. But, on the other hand, so was his duty as a doctor, to help those for whom medical aid was now imperative. He heard an enquiring voice close by him. Did he still intend to escape? He looked around and saw that it was Captain Tempez. Even before he replied, Dr. Mans realized that sub-consciously he had already made up his mind what his answer would be. He could not leave, ignoring the plight of those who lay injured around him. Tempez did not try to remonstrate with him, but replied that, he too, would stay and help.

The Doctor knelt by the woman on the ground. It transpired that the couple were husband and wife caught in the main hall during the bombing. A cursory examination was sufficient to show him that there was no chance of her surviving her serious injuries. Nevertheless, he determined to do what he could for her.

Sacrificing their chance to escape, a number of others had stopped behind to help the wounded, including Marius Couq. These men had much to lose by staying, but they came to Dr. Mans and offered to assist in any way they could. Dr. Mans knew where there was an operating table in the prison and he suggested that if it was undamaged it could be carried out into the courtyard. Starting with the woman, the injured were brought to the Doctor and carefully lifted onto the table for examination and treatment. There were many requiring immediate attention, and with the limited medical supplies available Dr. Mans and his volunteers worked on into the afternoon treating as many as they could locate. Nor were the wounded German guards excluded from their medical aid and care. Even the aggressive sole survivor of the patrol machine-gunned by the aircraft, who staggered around threatening everyone with his sub-machine gun, was calmed and bandaged by Dr. Mans. A new factor that hindered work in the courtyard was the stench and filth that flowed from a cesspool hit during the bombing.

By now, 437 prisoners had made good their escape through the breached walls. Some, like Jean Beaurin, had delayed their departure temporarily to search for missing friends or relatives. In the smoke and confusion it was an almost impossible task. In the end, Beaurin assumed that they had already escaped, and scrambled through the breach himself. Not until later was he to

Amiens prison 5 days after the air attack

KEY.

1 GAPS IN THE OUTER WALL
2 GUARDS ANNEXES ALMOST COMPLETELY DESTROYED
3 DEMOLISHED GUARDS QUARTERS IN MAIN BUILDING
4 DAMAGED WORKSHOPS
5 DAMAGED NORTHERN WING CONTAINING `POLITICAL PRISONERS´

learn that his brother had been killed and his mother wounded.

Although a good deal of the promised help and transport had not materialized in time for the attack, Ponchardier and his men, aided by a number of the local citizens, helped disperse and guide a great many of those escaping to safety. Ponchardier finally departed at 12.30 pm transporting some 30 prisoners away in a lorry. The past half-hour had been chaotic, but he had done all he could within the limits of his resources.

A final effort was made to try and induce Dr. Mans to leave, when at one o'clock a car arrived outside the prison to take him into hiding. People around him urged him to go whilst there was still time, but the Doctor emphatically refused to forsake those still in need of medical attention. Returning to his work he immediately set off to locate four German soldiers reported to be lying critically injured amid the ruins.

It was widely expected that by this time the Germans would have arrived to investigate the situation at the prison. But in fact it was almost two o'clock before they finally appeared. In their wake came the medical staff and relief teams of the Amiens Passive Defence movement. The lateness of their arrival could be attributed mainly to two things. At first, after the departure of the aircraft, the Germans and majority of the local populace had been deceived into thinking that the Mosquitos' diversion over the railway had been the main attack. They had made their way to the station area expecting to see signs of extensive bomb damage. They had remained puzzled by the lack of this until later, when it was learned that the prison on the outskirts of Amiens had been the target. Secondly, and ironically, the widest breach in the outer walls had been in a wall on the far side of the prison, out of sight of the town, and opening onto fields. Most of the prisoners had used this breach during their escape and were therefore not seen.

The relief teams of the Amiens Passive Defence set to work at once to dig the remaining injured out of the ruins. Equipped only with picks and shovels, they first had to manhandle out of the way great slabs of concrete and masonry. A detachment of patriots from these teams undertook a risky assignment, under the noses of the Germans. It was to remove the prisoners 'criminal records' from the ruined German offices.

The attitude of the Germans themselves was to concentrate on stepping up security, bringing in extra troops and police, and in general to ignore the rescue operations. With the reinforcements came the Amiens Gestapo, headed by Braumann, their chief. Some of their number infiltrated the rescue teams in the hope of discovering Resistance members working with them, whilst others carried out an identity inspection of the corpses laid out in a nearby shed.

While the German authorities organized a widespread search for the escaped prisoners, there was a great deal of coming and going outside the prison. Troops and police restrained a large crowd that had gathered at the front of the building, anxious for news. Ambulances began arriving to move the more seriously wounded to hospital, while the remaining prisoners were removed for safe custody to the fortress at Amiens. Meanwhile, inside the prison, the rescue teams feverishly worked to free the last of those buried in the debris. It was to be a further two days before this was accomplished.

For eight minutes Flight Lieutenant Tony Wickham flying the Film Production Unit's Mosquito DZ414 'O-Orange' had circled to the north of the prison. Now that the last of the attacking aircraft had left the target area, he commenced his run in. In addition to the aircraft's fixed cameras, the observer/photographer from his position in the specially glazed nose made his own photographic record of the scene below.

They saw clearly the crumbled walls and the smoking damaged buildings. But of major interest were the diminutive figures running along the roads and across the fields. Eventually, after the third pass, the enthusiastic cameraman was satisfied, much to the relief of Wickham, who knew that Focke-Wulf 190s were active in the area.

Pickard had already left the scene of operations, convinced by what he had seen of the success of the mission. Calling up the reserve squadron on the VHF radio, he instructed them to withdraw using the pre-arranged code words: 'Daddy from Dypeg. Red, red, red'. The crews of the four Mosquitos of 21 Squadron led by their Commanding Officer, Wing Commander I.G. 'Daddy' Dale, had patiently fulfilled their role as 'first reserve'. Any

disappointment they may have felt as non-participants evaporated when Pickard's voice over the radio announced that the attack had achieved its object. With their bomb loads intact and their Typhoon escort close by, they turned for home.

Meanwhile, preparatory to the return flight, the other squadrons were reforming near Albert.

The Typhoons had done an excellent job in keeping the Focke-Wulfs at bay. They had fought hard to stop the German fighter threat from developing during the attack on the prison, as well as providing close cover with their meagre numbers during the withdrawal. But the action had not been without loss to themselves. One of their number had been shot down near Amiens, but the pilot, a Canadian, had managed to forceland his aircraft in a field. Another Typhoon pilot had sustained battle damage to his aircraft which later proved fatal to him. Resuming his escort duties on the return flight, he was observed to climb into cloud over the Channel, after which he disappeared without trace.

In spite of the flak and FW 190s, the RAF had so far lost none of its Mosquitos through enemy action. But now the German anti-aircraft defences around Albert began taking a steady toll. In rapid succession two Mosquitos were hit and damaged. One of these, 'T-Tommy' a 487 Squadron aircraft flown by Pilot Officer M.N. Sparks, endured a difficult return trip after flak struck an engine and holed a wingtip. Putting down at the nearest south coast airfield, the flight ended when the aircraft skidded to a halt after the collapse of the undercarriage.

The Australian 464 Squadron suffered the next loss when MM404 flying at 50 feet was hit by a hail of light flak. Despite face and arm injuries, the pilot, Squadron Leader I.R. McRitchie, desperately fought to keep the aircraft airborne for as long as possible. His navigator, Flight Lieutenant R.W. Sampson, was dead beside him. A New Zealander, and ex-farmer, Sampson had been a popular figure in the Squadron and the second of two brothers to be killed in action in the RAF. The aircraft rapidly began to lose height but somehow McRitchie managed to effect a crash landing in the snow. He survived his injuries to become a Prisoner of War until the war ended.

Hawker Typhoon Mk. 1b., No.198 (Fighter) Squadron

Pickard, approaching Albert fast and at low level, had seen McRitchie go down and altered course to investigate, hoping to establish the fate of the crew. Turning north-easterly away from the remainder of the force who were now setting course for home, he too ran into ground fire which left one engine trailing a thin stream of smoke.

The lone Mosquito, now devoid of the protective fighter escort, became a vunerable target. It was at this moment that the aircraft was spotted and bounced by a pair of FW.190s. Although aware that German fighters were somewhere in the vicinity, Pickard and Broadley, their attention distracted by the search for McRitchie's aircraft, were taken completely by surprise. Pickard immediately took evasive action, but it was too late. Pressing home their attack, one of the Focke-Wulfs coming in astern of Pickard rapidly closed the range and opened fire with cannon and machine-guns.

A succession of explosions rocked the Mosquito as the concentrated fire crashed home. Instantly part of the tail unit broke away, filling the air with a mass of fluttering debris, then the nose dropped and the aircraft plummeted to the ground. The wreckage of 'F-Freddie' lay scattered over a snow-covered field near Montigny. There were no survivors. 'Pick' and 'Bill', the aerial partnership which had begun in the early days of the war and survived so many perilous missions, had endured to the end.

At Hunsdon, after the debriefing, feelings of elation over the success of the missions were tempered by the loss of the two crews. Word that the renowned Pickard was missing spread rapidly through the station, but for some time after the mission it was felt that somehow or other he would get back. Not until reconnaissance aircraft reported seeing his wrecked Mosquito and the French Resistance radioed the true facts did all hope finally die.

In Picardy, the intensive search by the Germans for the escaped prisoners was being ruthlessly carried out. At first, their efforts were rewarded and a considerable number were soon tracked down and recaptured. In addition to those retaken, there were others who, in fear of reprisals against their families, voluntarily gave themselves up. Out of the original 437 prisoners who had escaped, however, 255 remained free, much to the chagrin of the Occupation authorities and particularly of the Gestapo. Braumann and his agents persisted in their interrogations, especially amongst the men recaptured and the wounded in hospital, hoping to get a lead to the whereabouts of those still at large.

In Amiens cathedral a funeral service was held for the one hundred and two French dead. Conducting the service, Monsignor Martin, in his address to the congregation, alluded to 'this unforeseen and mysterious catastrophe'. An ironic touch was created by the representation of the Vichy French authorities at the service. They had hoped by their presence and sympathetic attitude to degrade the action of the RAF. These Nazi collaborators were, of course, in doing so, unwittingly paying homage to their bitter antagonists, the Resistance, whose members were numbered among the dead.

The bodies of Pickard and Broadley were removed from the wreckage of their Mosquito and reverently carried to the local church by villagers who had witnessed the crash. It had been their wish to honour the British airmen by carrying out the funeral arrangements themselves, but when the Germans arrived, the villagers, reluctantly and under protest, were forced to give them up. On the 19th, the Germans buried Pickard and Broadley in a cemetery close by the prison. Although expressly forbidden to do so by the authorities, the villagers attended the graveside to pay their last respects. When northern France was liberated later that year, a visit was paid by members of 140 Wing to the scene of the crash. They were told how their two colleagues had met their fate and shown the place where it had all ended. In the field, close to the still existing aircraft wreckage, a memorial in the shape of a large cross had been erected by the village. The personal belongings of the two airmen, removed at the time to prevent them from falling into the hands of the Gestapo, were taken from their place of safe keeping and, together with photographs of the flower-covered graves, handed over to their RAF comrades.

In the days immediately following the RAF attack on the prison, the citizens of Amiens were uneasy in their minds when they tried to reconcile the bombing with the facts as they knew them. To most, the true reasons behind the air operation were, of course, unknown. What was known so far was that it had made possible the escape of many of those imprisoned there. Apart from

Pickard's Mos

de HAVILLAND MOSQUITO Mk.VI
Fighter-Bomber of No. 487 Squadron, RNZ

HX922 EC·F

LEADING PARTICULARS

Length .... 40 ft. 10·75 in.

Wing Span .... 54 ft. 2 in.

Height (tail up) .... 17 ft. 5 in.

Wheel Track .... 16 ft. 4 in.

F◉EG HX922

Ft.

0   5

the casualties known to have been incurred, the question that caused most concern was why the prison wing holding captured Resistance members had been hit by the bombs. To people ignorant of the true facts, it was not unnatural in the circumstances to wonder if this had been part of some deliberate plan, following the recent mass arrests, to attempt to ensure their silence.

The truth, when it became generally known, dispelled for good all conjecture and rumour to this effect. The knowledge that the execution of Resistance leaders had been imminent, and that the organization itself had planned and requested the raid, fully accepting the consequences, had the effect of putting things into their proper perspective. When returning rescue team members reported on the method and general accuracy of the bombing, admiration replaced doubt when it was then realized how difficult had been the airmen's task, and how small their margin of error. Although innocent people had been among the victims of this urgent operation to save life, their deaths were not in vain. Their sacrifice, too, had been for their country. An additional and hitherto unknown factor had also come to light. When the guard at the prison had been reinforced by German troops, following the abortive St. Quentin prison rescue attempt, they had brought with them a stock of grenades which had been stored within the compound. These too had contributed to the general destruction when they were detonated by the aircraft's bombs.

A message from the French underground radio network was received in London five days after the air operation. It thanked the RAF in the name of the Resistance for carrying out the attack and commended them on the 'admirable precision' of their bombing. Their first bombs, it stated, had blown in nearly all the cell doors. The message went on to say that, although they had not been able to save all the prisoners, many, aided by the local population, had made good their escape, including twelve who were to have been shot the next day. It also made reference to the 'violence' of the bombing, and the delayed action of the bombs being too short. There had not been enough time for the prisoners to take cover. Not all the casualties had been caused by the bombs, it confirmed, 'some had been killed by German machine-

Table of Mosquitos taking part in the mission. (Positions of individual aircraft are not necessarily authentic. Where known, aircraft serial numbers have been included.)

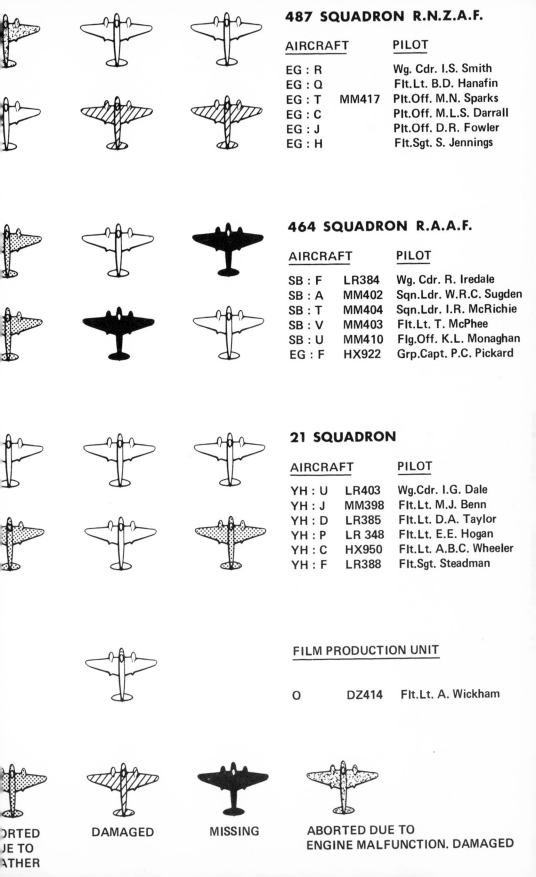

487 SQUADRON R.N.Z.A.F.

AIRCRAFT		PILOT
EG : R		Wg. Cdr. I.S. Smith
EG : Q		Flt.Lt. B.D. Hanafin
EG : T	MM417	Plt.Off. M.N. Sparks
EG : C		Plt.Off. M.L.S. Darrall
EG : J		Plt.Off. D.R. Fowler
EG : H		Flt.Sgt. S. Jennings

464 SQUADRON R.A.A.F.

AIRCRAFT		PILOT
SB : F	LR384	Wg. Cdr. R. Iredale
SB : A	MM402	Sqn.Ldr. W.R.C. Sugden
SB : T	MM404	Sqn.Ldr. I.R. McRichie
SB : V	MM403	Flt.Lt. T. McPhee
SB : U	MM410	Flg.Off. K.L. Monaghan
EG : F	HX922	Grp.Capt. P.C. Pickard

21 SQUADRON

AIRCRAFT		PILOT
YH : U	LR403	Wg.Cdr. I.G. Dale
YH : J	MM398	Flt.Lt. M.J. Benn
YH : D	LR385	Flt.Lt. D.A. Taylor
YH : P	LR 348	Flt.Lt. E.E. Hogan
YH : C	HX950	Flt.Lt. A.B.C. Wheeler
YH : F	LR388	Flt.Sgt. Steadman

FILM PRODUCTION UNIT

O	DZ414	Flt.Lt. A. Wickham

ORTED
JE TO
ATHER   DAMAGED   MISSING   ABORTED DUE TO
ENGINE MALFUNCTION. DAMAGED

guns'. The message ended on a congratulatory note: 'To sum up', it read, 'it was a success'.

Soon the tide of battle in Europe overtook the recent events in Amiens, and other operations became the focal point of the military strategists. For security reasons, details of the air operation were not released to the British Press or public until the October of that year. But in France, the long term issues that followed as a direct result of Operation 'Jericho' had only just begun.

Now it was the turn of the invader to feel despair as the prolonged hunt for the escaped prisoners continued. For, as the Germans well knew, many of those who had managed to avoid recapture, were in a position to identify Gestapo counter-espionage agents who had given evidence against them at their recent trials. By contacting the Resistance movement without delay, these men, at great personal risk, were able to expose at least sixty of these German informers. The outcome of this was to render the enemy counter-espionage network in the area almost totally ineffective. In turn, this resulted in the number of arrests being immediately reduced, thus giving the Resistance organiz-ation in the Somme region the respite that it so badly needed.

Perhaps the most important single contribution made by the raid was the effect that the operation had on French morale. It showed that Britain had not forgotten the part being played by the secret armies of her Allies in the occupied countries of Europe. News of the special low-level daylight attack quickly spread from region to region, bringing to the Resistance fighters the fresh strength born of reassurance that help was at hand.

But what of the men who participated in he prison drama on that bleak February morning?

The stalwart Ponchardier, orginator of the operation, continued his dangerous fight, his resourcefulness and guile keeping him one step ahead of the Germans until the day of liberation. In recognition of his services to his country, he was justly awarded the *Croix de la Libération.*

Not all the prisoners escaping that day did so without difficulty. One for whom things went wrong was M. Raymond Vivant; after leaving the breach in the wall, he did not, as he had hoped, get to

Albert. Learning that German forces were on the road somewhere ahead of him, he turned about and retraced his steps in the direction of Amiens — but when he reached the outskirts of the town he ran into trouble. At a crossroads not far from the prison he was stopped and arrested by German troops. Fortunately, luck was still on his side. By subterfuge he successfully evaded his guards and for the second time that day regained his liberty. For some time he continued to elude his captors until eventually he was able to make contact with the Resistance.

Dr. Mans, and all the other prisoners who had stopped behind to help the wounded, had in the meantime been interned in the fortress at Amiens. To the Doctor's friends, the Gestapo Chief Braumann professed admiration for the conduct and work of the Doctor and his helpers. He readily gave assurances that the German authorities would always recognise and reward courageous actions such as these. The fact that they had saved German as well as French lives would weigh heavily in their favour. It was certain, he said, that Dr. Mans' release from the fortress would shortly be arranged. It was also hoped that others who had remained behind might earn similar or at least more lenient treatment.

Alas, nothing could have been further from the truth. Dr. Mans spent several more weeks at the fortress and then suddenly he was transferred to Royallieu, a camp near Compiègne. Then in May 1944 he was deported to Germany. In the months that followed he was moved from camp to camp, spending the cruel winter of 1944-45 in terrible conditions at a labour camp at Fallersleben. The decimated survivors were transported from there in the following spring to another camp at Weobelin in Mecklenburg, where many more were to die. The Allied advance in the invasion of Europe had now gained momentum and was rapidly over-running this area. On the 2nd of May 1945, American forces arrived and liberated the camp. Among the wretched inmates who still remained alive was Dr. Mans.

In October 1944, just outside the town of Arras, a mass grave was discovered under a mount covered with tall grass. It contained 260 bodies, victims of German executioners. Among the remains identified were those of Captain Tempez and most of the men who had sacrificed their freedom to help the wounded in the

prison courtyard on February 18th. There had, after all, been no clemency shown, for it was subsequently proved that they had been shot only two months after the raid.

Operation 'Jericho' was a bold undertaking and was not without its critics on both sides of the channel. The ethics involved in requesting and mounting the operation have been questioned and argued over many times. However, when viewed in the context of the times and the conditions then prevailing, there can surely be little room for doubting its validity and urgency. The Somme region in 1944 was suffering badly from the miseries of German oppression. The existence of its one instrument of retaliation, the Resistance Movement, had become endangered. Desperate measures were called for, and duly taken; the loss of life incurred, both French and British, although regrettable, was part of the risk accepted in order to achieve the success of the mission.

The attack on the prison became a forerunner of similar operations to be carried out at the request of Resistance organizations in Europe. The low-level, pin-point bombing of selected targets such as SS Barracks and Gestapo Headquarters soon became a speciality of No.2 Groups Mosquito Squadrons.

On the morning of the mission Charles Pickard had ended his briefing of the assembled aircrews with these words: 'It's a death or glory job, boys. You have to break that prison wide open'. It was to prove a strangely prophetic statement. The prison was opened, but Pickard, among others who flew that day, was destined not to return.

The French people, however, did not forget the courage of Pickard and the RAF crews. In 1945 a memorial was erected at Amiens as a tribute to them. Embedded in it are parts of Pickard's Mosquito salvaged from the wreckage. It remains one of the few relics left to commemorate this desperate and historic mission.

Squadron crests of No.140 Wing

OPERATION THUNDERBOLT

OPERATION THUNDERBOLT

The two Spitfires flying low over the English Channel, spotted two Messerschmitts and decided to attack, the time 10.26 am, February 12th, 1942. It seemed to the British pilots as they raced to meet their adversaries just a normal encounter. The weather was typical of February, low rain clouds, white tops to the waves below — when you could see them.

In the ensuing dogfight, the Spitfire pilots suddenly became aware that more and more German fighters were attacking them. Then, to their amazement, they saw the brown puffs of anti-aircraft shells bursting around them.

They both dived through the low clouds and on emerging were astonished to see three German capital ships steaming up the Channel, surrounded by a screen of destroyers and outside them a further screen of fast E-boats or MTBs. The anti-aircraft guns on all the ships began putting up a formidable barrage which the two Spitfires flew through, missing the tops of the waves by only a few feet as they levelled out of their dive.

This was no place for two lonely Spitfires. Both pilots headed for home, keeping low over the water until they reached the white cliffs of the English coast. It was not until they landed and were debriefed by their Squadron Intelligence Officer — twelve hours after the German ships had left Brest harbour — that the escape of the German Squadron, a little armada, became known to the shocked British authorities.

The Prelude

After the 'Battle of Britain' in 1940, Hitler decided to throw the might of the German army against Russia. All the French-based Luftwaffe squadrons that could be spared were transferred to the Russian front. In the early stages of the campaign things went smoothly for him. His troops advanced well into Russia, until late in 1941. Then the Wehrmacht ground to a halt, for so rapid had been their advance that the vital supplies required for an army to operate had not been able to keep up with them. Also the Russian winter was setting in, and the clothing worn by the troops was no

F

match for its rigours. It looked as though they would have to face a hard winter campaign without the proper means to fight it.

It was during the latter half of 1941 that the British launched a series of commando raids on coastal targets in Norway. Between August 25th and September 3rd, the coal mines at Spitzbergen were put out of action. At the same time the British evacuated both the Norwegian and Russian populations of the port. On December 27th the Vaagso Island was raided. This time 16,000 tons of shipping were destroyed, and all the coastal batteries put out of action. The raiders took 98 prisoners back with them.

With British attacks all along the Norwegian seaboard, and constant intelligence reports warning Hitler of a possible attempt by the British to open a second front, the Fuehrer decided to strengthen his naval forces in these waters. To do this meant transferring some of his capital ships from their present stations. It was the logical answer to the problem, for he could not afford to become sandwiched between the British on one side and the Russians on the other. What he did not know — and neither did the Russians — was that the British at this particular point of the war were not in a position to open up a second front. Neither were they able to supply Russia with the vast amount of aid she was demanding.

One cannot blame Hitler if he thought these raids by the British commandos were a prelude to invasion. His famous 'intuition' was working overtime, with just cause. It was this same intuition that told him to move his ships out of the port of Brest. There were three capital ships at that time in Brest, *Scharnhorst*, *Gneisenau* and *Prinz Eugen*. The first two were battle cruisers of 32,000 tons, armed with nine 28-cm and twelve 15-cm guns, while the latter was a cruiser of 13,900 tons, armed with eight 20.3-cm and twelve 10.5-cm guns. These three ships between them had sunk over a million tons of British shipping, including the aircraft carrier *Glorious*. If the British could keep them bottled up in Brest, it was to their advantage, and to this end they had set up constant surveillance of the German ships by both aircraft and submarines. The ships also came under regular air attack from the RAF. Although the British had not yet developed their 'Grand Slam' bomb, they did have armour piercing bombs which could

Scharnhorst

Prinze Eugen

Top:— The Gneisenau   Bottom:— Destroyer Z33 in Norwegian waters

penetrate the heavy armour plating of the ships' decks, and were a constant nuisance, causing a great deal of damage to the superstructure of the ships and harbour installations.

So, with the transfer of these ships in mind, Hitler sent for Grand Admiral Raeder; this was unfortunate for Raeder, who was planning an extended cruise for these ships in the Atlantic. He had hoped to have the ships seaworthy by March or April of 1942 and once again doing the job for which they had been built, attacking Allied shipping on the high seas. As Hitler unfolded his plan to him, Raeder had to agree that the Norwegian waters did need their defences strengthened. He suggested to Hitler that the *Tirpitz* could do it single-handed, leaving his plans for the Brest squadron unhampered. And he did not think it advisable to take three of Germany's capital ships up the Channel in broad daylight, as Hitler's plan implied. This in his opinion would be courting disaster. Hitler was furious. He told Raeder if he could not have his orders obeyed he would dismantle the three ships in Brest, and use their guns for coastal defence in Norway. Raeder did not think the British would invade Norway, but it was no use arguing. So with a heavy heart and much misgiving, he went back to his desk and set about making plans for the transfer of the ships.

It was obvious that the key to the whole operation was air supremacy. The man to help him here was Major General Hans Jeschonnek, Chief of the Luftwaffe General Staff. Raeder explained the situation to Jeschonnek, who in turn asked his newly appointed C-in-C of the German Fighter Arm, Adolf Galland, to come with him to the next meeting to be held at Hitler's HQ in East Prussia. This was to be Galland's first big job as 'General of the Fighter Arm'.

Galland, one of Germany's ace fighter pilots, had been promoted from commanding a squadron. He had succeeded Werner Molders, killed in a flying accident. The state of the fighter arm when Galland took command was weak. Replacement aircraft seldom reached the Luftwaffe squadrons based in France; most of them went to the Russian front. It was Hitler's belief that the French based bomber squadrons could deal with the British. Production of fighter aircraft had been relegated to second place after the Battle of Britain, on the express orders of Hitler.

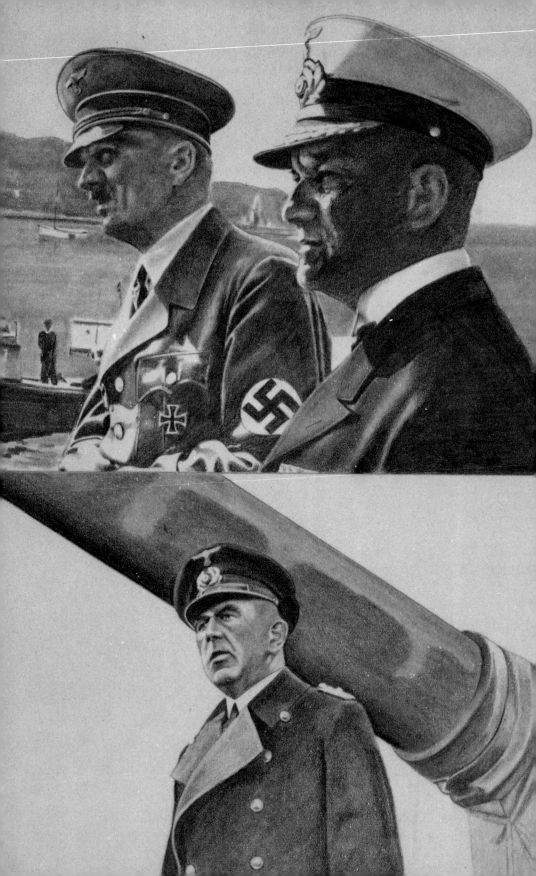

Bombers were given top priority. Once the Fuehrer issued the order, nobody could make him change his mind, not even Göring. And to the last, Hitler would maintain that his fighter arm had let him down in the Battle of Britain.

So it was that when Jeschonnek and Galland attended the next meeting in the 'Wolf's Lair', Hitler's bunker headquarters, they knew that they would be hard pressed to give Hitler the air umbrella he required for his capital ships. In attendance also were Admiral Raeder, Vice Admiral Ciliax and Commodore Ruge — the two latter being senior officers of the naval squadron at Brest — other members of the HQ staff and, of course, the Fuehrer himself.

It was Ciliax who explained the three-point plan that had been drawn up by the Admiralty Staff. It was simple:

1. The movement of ships to be reduced to a minimum before the operation.
2. The ships must leave the port of Brest at night, in order to traverse the Channel in daylight.
3. The ships must have the strongest fighter escort between dawn and dusk.

Hitler himself emphasised this last point. The Luftwaffe must play the decisive part in this operation. Jeschonnek pointed out that with only 250 fighters at his disposal, things might not be all that easy. To give adequate air protection to the ships over the period required, he argued that he would need more aircraft. He thought he could meet the requirements by using 30 night fighters during the early hours of the morning, and again in the evening.

Raeder agreed that if Jeschonnek's analysis was correct more aircraft were needed, and asked also that the British torpedo aircraft bases should be raided. Hitler concurred, and issued an order freeing some of the fighter squadrons of the German home defence units. He would not allow any to be released from the Russian front.

The conference ended with a summary by Hitler, outlining the main points. The ships were to depart at night from Brest, using the surprise factor to its utmost by passing Dover at noon, disregarding the fears of his Admiralty staff that once the British found out what was happening they would transfer large

Top: Hitler and Raeder   Bottom: Ciliax

squadrons of fighter and bomber aircraft to the south coast of England — he did not think the British capable of making quick decisions. Finally he begged for the utmost secrecy concerning the operation. Only those present at the meeting would know the actual plans. Even so, Hitler had a special document in the form of a pledge prepared and made all those present sign it. Nobody outside that select few would be told of the plans until the last minute, and then only if it should be deemed absolutely necessary.

After the meeting was over and everyone had signed Hitler's pledge of secrecy, the Fuehrer drew Galland aside and asked him if he thought the operation could succeed. Choosing his words carefully, Galland gave what he thought to be his honest opinion. He told Hitler that there were two things needed for the success of the operation — surprise and luck. One thing he could promise his leader was that the men under his command would give of their best, the rest was up to the gods.

The Preparation

Directly the meeting ended preparations started, for there was a great deal to be done. The Luftwaffe would not come under the command of the Navy during this operation, but would work in close co-operation with it. Right from the start, however, a spirit of camaraderie prevailed between both services, and it proved to be one of the most successful combined operations the Germans ever carried out.

The chain of command for the operation was as follows:
1. The Naval High Command gave the order for the operation.
2. Two Operational Commands — Naval Group West and Naval Group North — would share command responsibility, for the ships would be passing from one command to the other. Naval Group West had its headquarters in Paris and operated between Brest and the Scheldt Estuary. Naval Group North, with headquarters at Kiel, operated from the Scheldt up to and including Norwegian waters.
3. Vice Admiral Ciliax was in command of the battleships, under the authority of the respective Naval Command HQ whose waters he was in at the time.

Ciliax inspects his men aboard 'Scharnhorst'

4. The Captains of the three main ships concerned in the operation were Captain Hoffman of the *Sharnhorst.*, Captain Fein of the *Gneisenau* and Captain Brinkmann of the *Prinz Eugen*

By special 'Order of the Fuehrer', Adolf Galland was made responsible for the preparation and control of fighter protection, the 'air umbrella' over the ships.

Two code names were chosen for the operation, 'Thunderbolt' for the air arm and 'Cerberus' for the navy. This was a security measure, to create an impression of two operations instead of one. The whole operational planning got under way. In naval circles everyone was led to believe that the ships would shortly be putting to sea for a long Atlantic voyage, while the fighter arm was supposed to be getting ready to carry out a large scale offensive against British sea ports and radar installations. Many false radio messages were sent out, in the knowledge that the enemy would certainly pick them up. The Fuehrer himself said he was going to feed the enemy with news that the ships would be sailing for Pacific waters to help the Japanese. He quipped that the quickest way of passing this information to the enemy would be to tell his Italian partner. Whether he did or not remains a mystery. Other ways were also found to fool the enemy, such as issuing tropical kit to the sailors and having drums of oil stacked on the dockside at Brest for the French dockers to see — with the words 'For tropical use only' painted on their sides.

The serious planning was going on in the headquarters of each command, behind closed doors. Galland for his part was trying to work out a rota for his 280 aircraft. It was important that the ships should have as many aircraft as possible over them at any given moment on their journey. At the same time he must keep an adequate reserve. The night fighters would only be used in the early hours of dawn, and again at dusk. They would not be used during the day. These aircraft were Me.110s fitted with special night interception radar. The other aircraft at Galland's disposal were some of the best fighter planes of their day — Me.109s and FW.190s. There was not much in the enemy's air force that could outfly them, and the young men who were piloting them had every confidence in their machines.

Messerschmitt BF109F

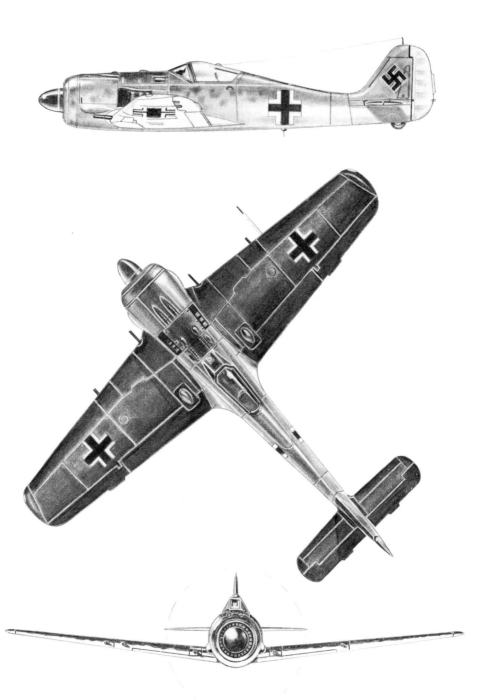

Galland divided his units up into flights of sixteen. Each unit was to cover the ships for approximately half an hour, a period governed by the amount of fuel the aircraft could carry. There was to be an overlap of 10 to 15 minutes as each flight came into the other's patrol area, therefore for that period of time the ships would have the protection of 32 aircraft. It was something like a relay race, with the sixteen-plane fighter flights passing the baton to each other all the way up the Channel. It was a simple plan. The first group of planes, with headquarters at Caen, would escort from Cherbourg to Abbeville. The second group was based at Le Touquet, and would escort the ships from Abbeville to Calais. The third sector was between Calais and the Zuider Zee, with its HQ at Schiphol. The fourth and final sector, with its HQ at Jever, covered the sector Zuider Zee to Wilhemshaven.

As soon as it was time for a fighter group to leave the ships, they would land, reservice and be ready to go again when required. Meanwhile, other units, complete with ground crews, were transferred to Galland's command from the Reich and 3rd Air Force Groups.

It was important that the fighters should be controlled from the ships themselves, and for this purpose Galland inaurgurated what he called his 'fighter command afloat'. Their HQ was on board the flagship *Scharnhorst*, with Oberst Ibel in charge of liaison. With him were fighter pilots of the first and second fighter sections. In charge of radio personnel was Oberst Elle. This was the size of the staff of the 'fighter command afloat' headquarters. Each of the other ships had a pilot officer and a radio operator aboard. Galland was linked to the ships by longwave radio from each of his headquarters, while the ships were linked to each other and the aircraft protecting them by shortwave radio.

Next came the ships' work-out trials at sea. These trials were carried out by the ships individually and in pairs, on each occasion they had a fighter escort. They took place between January 22nd and February 10th 1942, and there were eight sea trials in all. The fighters flew a total of 450 sorties, during which a few enemy aircraft who came to investigate the movement of the ships were shot down. Everything went well, and a great team spirit developed between the Navy and Luftwaffe. Even so, Galland's

Focke-Wulf FW190A

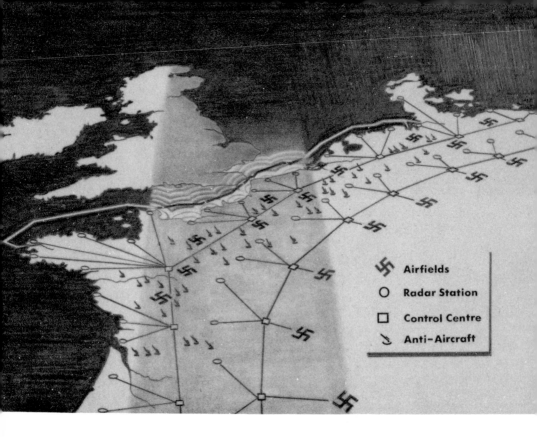

Legend:

卐 Airfields
○ Radar Station
☐ Control Centre
↘ Anti–Aircraft

Top: Showing German anti-radar and airfields — Bottom: German 'E' boat

pilots covering these trials did not know that they were rehearsals for an actual operation. Never once during the trials did the British make a sustained attack on the ships at sea.

Gradually Galland was getting his units organised, linking each airfield to his HQs by means of ultra-shortwave radio. He was also going to be able to monitor the progress of the ships up-Channel on the radar screens in each of his headquarters.

The Luftwaffe had as head of its electronics section General Martini, whose official title was 'Chief of Communications and Intelligence'. He was asked to develop a device which would be capable of jamming the radar stations on the opposite side of the Channel. Although he could not guess the purpose of this request he set about the invention of a new device; it was not long before the British noticed they were getting interference on their radar screens. At first they must have thought something was wrong with their radar sets, for the interference occurred only during short periods of time. Martini was able to tell Galland that he could have continuous radar jamming for as long as he wanted from the beginning of February, with radar-jamming stations set up at Cherbourg, Dieppe, Boulogne and Ostend. Even so, Galland could not afford to put all his faith in this new and untried invention. If it operated as hoped, and the ships did manage to slip up the Channel undetected by the British coastal radar, he knew it was only buying time.

The naval side of the preparations was well under way by now. Minesweepers had been sweeping a channel for the big ships to sail through, clearing in all 119 mines, 21 of which were land types. Navigation was being worked out to give the ships at least 15 fathoms, the minimum depth required to allow them to steam at maximum speed in safety. The route plotted would take them as close inshore on the French side of the Channel as possible. This would allow for picking up survivors in the event of any of the ships being sunk. Marker boats were to be used along the route as aids to navigation.

Only the fixing of the actual date of the operation now remained. To do this, many factors had to be taken into account, the state of the weather, the moon, the length of the night. It was important to move the ships in as many hours of darkness as possible, which would give the enemy little daylight to attack in. The condition of the moon was important also, for a full moon could provide the enemy with enough light to carry on the battle well into the hours of darkness. Cloud would be helpful, of course, but a storm would be even better, with plenty of low clouds. This would not help Galland's pilots either, but the ships would benefit.

To enable the meteorologists to make an accurate forecast, weather conditions in the Atlantic were reported daily by three U-boats specially stationed there for the purpose. Long range reconnaissance planes stationed on the west coast of France also gave regular reports on the weather. Gradually the information was collected, until the met men were able to promise a favourable set of conditions to the Commander-in-Chief of the West Navy Group. A depression forming to the south of Ireland, moving south east slowly, would give the weather conditions required for the operation. This information was passed on to Admiral Saahwachter, Commander-in-Chief, West Navy Group Command. The period the meteorologists recommended was February 10th–15th. After due consideration, Admiral Saahwachter decided 20.000 hours on the night of 11th February (Continental time) as the departure time for the ships.

The Green Light

Colonel Galland, who had been at an all day conference in Paris, left for his Headquarters in the Pas de Calais. He had summoned all his squadron leaders to a final conference before the operation began. On arrival he explained 'Thunderbolt' Operation, and for the first time his staff knew what their role was to be. After he had finished, each man was given an envelope containing sealed orders, to be opened by them on return to their units.

Galland had previously issued a directive to the squadrons setting out a set of regulations for the protection of shipping. This had been ostensibly a general directive which all pilots understood to refer to *merchant* shipping, but it was equally applicable to the ships of the Brest Squadron. The points made by Galland were these:

1. The safety of the ships being escorted was of the utmost importance.
2. Should it be found that enemy aircraft had penetrated the protection of the air umbrella, they were to be rammed.
3. No fighter pilots was to be drawn into an air combat which would lure him away from the ships.
4. It was important for all pilots to stay close to the ships at all times.
5. Should the enemy outnumber the Luftwaffe, reserves would be called in.

At last the pilots understood the significance of the directive, which had made no sense if applied to the protection of merchant shipping only.

That night there was much celebrating in the mess halls of the squadrons, for this was going to be an operation that would reinstate them in the eyes of their Fuehrer. Now they would be able to show him that they had not let him down during the Battle of Britain. Not many of the pilots slept that night.

The Channel Dash

On the night of February 11th, preparations began in Brest harbour to make the ships ready for departure. The great camouflage nets were removed and stowed in large heaps on the quayside. Telephone and other connecting lines to the jetty were removed, and as the hour for departure arrived, the small tugs came alongside to help the big ships out of harbour. The three ships already had a good head of steam in their boilers. They were about to cast off the big steel hawser cables, when suddenly the air raid sirens sounded.

The enemy could not have come at a worse time. There were the ships ready to leave, with all camouflage stripped, easy targets and at their most vulnerable. The smoke screen devices around the harbour started churning out a heavy protective cover, but had the enemy noticed the state of the ships?

Overhead the aircraft could be heard, and soon the whistle of bombs falling told the crews of the ships they were in for another heavy raid. Gradually, the haze of the smoke screen over the

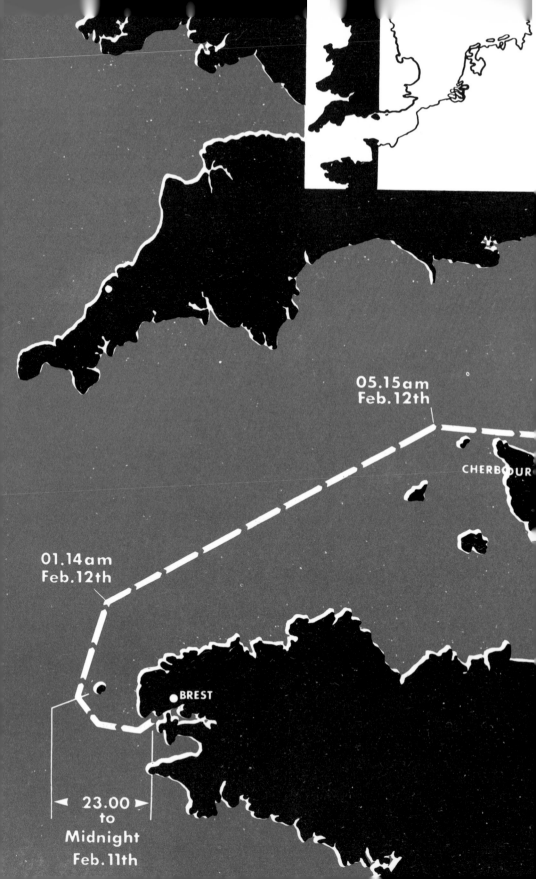

05.15am
Feb.12th

CHERBOUR

01.14am
Feb.12th

BREST

23.00
to
Midnight
Feb.11th

harbour smothered the ships in its protective shawl. By this time, the anti-aircraft guns were putting up a heavy barrage. These guns, both ship and shore based were very effective in spite of the smoke screen.

Although the British did considerable damage to the harbour installations, not one of the ships was hit. Twenty-five aircraft of RAF Bomber Command took part in the raid, one of them taking the usual reconnaissance photographs. On return to their base, these photographs showed that the ships were still tied up at their usual berths.

It was nearly two hours before the 'all-clear' was sounded on the sirens. Once again the ships prepared to leave, the time now nearly 22.00 hours.

The *Scharnhorst* was the first to sail. Due to the heavy smoke-screen, it was difficult for Captain Hoffmann to see the harbour entrance or the marker buoys at the ends of the main torpedo nets guarding the entrance to the harbour. When, out of the fog, one of the buoys did loom up, Hoffman discovered the *Scharnhorst* to be on the wrong side of it. The ship was slowly advancing over the top of the netting. Unless the engines were stopped, there was a good chance of the ship fouling the netting with her propellers, putting her out of the operation. Hoffmann ordered all engines 'Stop', and as the giant ship slid over the top of the net, the crew below decks could hear it slithering and scratching along the bottom of the ship. Eventually the noise ceased, much to everyone's relief, and the engines started again, their vibrations being felt throughout the ship as she built up speed. There were almost two hours to be made up before the whole careful jigsaw of planning could be complete and the operation workable.

Next out of harbour came *Gneisenau* She made it without incident, but *Prinz Eugen* was not so lucky. As she was being edged away from the jetty by one of her tugs, the cable from the tug to the ship became entangled in the ship's starboard propeller. Divers went down to investigate the damage, which was eventually cleared and the cruiser was able to leave harbour.

Outside the harbour, the ships formed up in line astern, while their escorting destroyers took positions on either flank. The

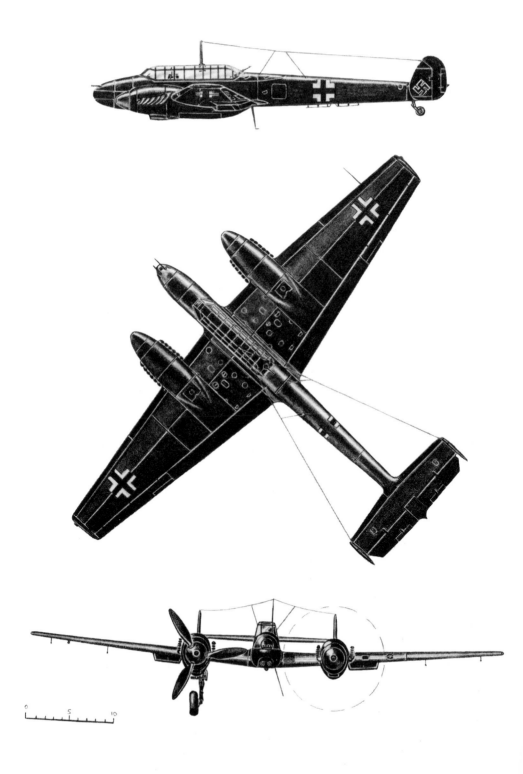

accompanying tugs had been ordered to maintain a course off Brest until noon next day, when they were supposed to pick up the ships again as they entered harbour. This, of course, was a security ruse, for the tugs had French crews.

The ships were now heading out into the Atlantic. After about fifteen minutes' sailing, the heading was changed to bring them on to their true course up Channel. It was a surprise to most of the ships' crews, for they did not know exactly what was happening, whether they were in fact out on gun firing trials or going on an operational mission into the Atlantic. Now, with the ships heading towards the English Channel, they were completely surprised. The time was nearly midnight, when suddenly the ships' loudspeakers burst into life, calling for the attention of all crew members. It was Admiral Ciliax speaking, and he explained the whole operation to the men, ending by wishing everyone 'Good Luck'. The reaction from the ships' crews at the news was electrifying, shouts and cheers could be heard from every quarter of the ships. Feelings of relief at leaving the constantly bombed port of Brest were mixed with wonder at the idea of such an audacious operation.

Steadily the ships ploughed on through the night, keeping up maximum speed of 30 knots in order to catch up with their time schedule; they must be half-way between Cherbourg and Le Havre by dawn. Just off Cherbourg, the first of the torpedo boats joined the convoy. They would in turn be relieved by another flotilla later on. Then the ships' loudspeakers called 'Clear for action – all hands to battle stations'. A peaceful night was coming to an end.

Meanwhile, at the first airfield, Galland's crews were getting into their Me.110 night fighters. One after another the engines of the aircraft burst into life as the pilots did their ground runs, checking both engines and instruments. Slowly they taxied from their dispersal points, ready for take-off. Four aircraft took off, climbing steadily into the blackness. The time was 8.14 am as they headed for the ships. At 8.50 am they spotted the ships, right where they should be, for the time lost had now been made up. Complete radio silence was in force, so as the planes approached, the leading pilot gave the visual recognition signal by firing two coloured Verey lights.

Oberstleutnant Hentschel, fighter controller in *Scharnhorst*,

Me 110 Night Fighter

heard the noise of their engines in the distance from his position in the crow's nest of the ship. The aircraft were approaching from the rear of the convoy, and it was a relief to him when he made out their familiar shapes through his night glasses. The ships' crews were even more relieved when they saw the black and white crosses painted under the wings of the aircraft as they flew low overhead. There was something satisfying in having friends flying above, guarding you, and Galland's pilots enjoyed being there as much as the ships crews were glad to have them.

Dawn had now come and gone, with the sun producing a typical sailors' warning of a sunrise. Visibility was good, and there were fast-moving, high-flying clouds, that promised to make the met reports come true. Everything was going well for the ships, almost too well. The main thought in every mind as the ships forged up Channel — in broad daylight now — was that they might be falling into a trap set by the British. It was too peaceful, 'Rather like a cruise', as one of the ships officers put it.

By 11.00 am the night fighters were due to be relieved by the first wing of day fighters. Constant radar jamming had already started at 9.0 am, as Martini had ordered. Martini's men tuned in to each known British radar station along the South coast. The British tried new wave lengths to avoid the jamming, but without avail.

The air umbrella was now up to full strength, the aircraft keeping low, flying up and down along the port side of the ships, between them and the enemy coast. The night fighters had returned to the nearest airfield on the Dutch sector to refuel and re-service, ready to join the ships again at dusk. Their part in the morning's journey had been uneventful. Now it was up to the day fighters, the Me.109s and Focke-Wulf 190s. These pilots had been briefed to fly as low as possible and to maintain radio silence until ordered otherwise. Galland was a little worried about the latter, for he knew his pilots to be notorious for breaking radio discipline. He need not have worried, for this time the pilots were fully aware of the importance of keeping quiet.

As well as the fighters patrolling the ships, Galland had dispersed on different airfields along the French coast between 25 and 30 aircraft on standby readiness. The pilots sat in these

German Fighter Pilots awaiting signal to 'Scramble'

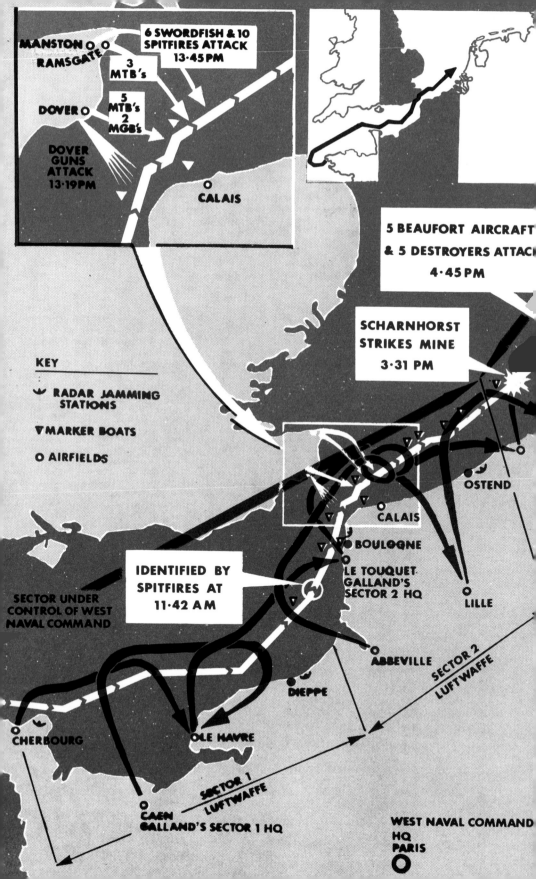

6 SWORDFISH & 10 SPITFIRES ATTACK 13·45 PM

MANSTON O O
RAMSGATE

3 MTB's

DOVER O

5 MTB's 2 MGB's

DOVER GUNS ATTACK 13·19 PM

CALAIS

5 BEAUFORT AIRCRAFT & 5 DESTROYERS ATTACK 4·45 PM

SCHARNHORST STRIKES MINE 3·31 PM

KEY

〰 RADAR JAMMING STATIONS

▽ MARKER BOATS

O AIRFIELDS

OSTEND

CALAIS

O BOULOGNE

IDENTIFIED BY SPITFIRES AT 11·42 AM

LE TOUQUET GALLAND'S SECTOR 2 HQ

LILLE

SECTOR UNDER CONTROL OF WEST NAVAL COMMAND

ABBEVILLE

SECTOR 2 LUFTWAFFE

DIEPPE

CHERBOURG

O LE HAVRE

SECTOR 1 LUFTWAFFE

O CAEN GALLAND'S SECTOR 1 HQ

WEST NAVAL COMMAND HQ PARIS
O

aircraft awaiting the call to action. During the morning they must have found it boring, and wondered where the action was. Later in the day they would have plenty, for their duty did not tie them to the ships alone; theirs was the freedom of the sky, to seek and destroy.

The ships by this time had reached the mouth of the Somme, only 40 miles from the narrowest point in the Channel, and still the British had made no attempt to intercept them. Had they in fact prepared some crushing countermeasure which would destroy the whole convoy? Was this silence only the calm before the storm? How could it be that German warships had been allowed to sail the hallowed waters of the English Channel unchallenged.

To the pilots flying escort with the ships, it was uneventful. They patrolled up and down, skimming low over the water. Flying over water can be very deceptive, judging height very difficult. Some of the pilots flew a little in advance of the ships, and it was these advance pilots who first came into contact with the enemy. The time was a little after eleven, when suddenly out of the clouds two Spitfires emerged. Galland's pilots immediately went to intercept them, but the Spitfire pilots, seeing the odds against them, quickly dived down to sea level, passing through one of the heaviest anti-aircraft barrages they must ever have faced, for it seemed as if all the ships had their guns trained on them. The pilots of the Spitfires could not help but notice the three capital ships in the convoy, and from the bridge of *Scharnhorst* Ciliax commented that the action would soon be starting. Strangely enough it was neither of these British pilots who first raised the alarm. The German listening service, constantly on the alert for British radio messages, picked up a message from the pilot of an unidentified aircraft, saying he had 'Just seen a large German naval force moving up Channel towards Dover at high speed, consisting of three capital ships and about twenty destroyers and MTBs'.

Urgently Galland debated whether to allow his pilots to break radio silence. He wisely decided against doing this. There was no sense in confirming that unknown British pilot's report. As it turned out, a whole hour passed before the enemy started to attack the ships. About midday the coastal guns at Dover opened fire. By this time the weather was closing in on the ships, which

had now reached the narrowest point in the Channel, the Straits of Dover. The famous white cliffs could not be seen from seaward, and the costal gunners had to fire blind. Galland's pilots could see the splashes as the shells entered the water, mostly near the *Prinz Eugen*. No hits were scored, and it was not long before the German coastal batteries opened up in reply.

With the ships about to pass Dover, and move out into the wider part of the Channel, time was running out for the British. Off Boulogne the convoy was joined by fifteen more E-boats, which took up positions on the port flank of the ships. Still no sight of a British attack. Then ahead of the ships, Ciliax heard some gunfire, and was told that enemy MTBs were engaging his forward MTBs. These proved to be boats from Dover, first spotted by Fw.190 pilots, who flew low over them. They did not engage the enemy boats, however, preferring to save their ammunition for later engagements with the RAF.

Just about this time, Admiral Ciliax was handed a message that had been picked up by the German Intelligence Service, the *B-Dienst*, and decoded. It was a message from one of the enemy MTBs to the British Admiralty in Whitehall, giving definite confirmation that there were German battleships in the Straits of Dover. The time was now 12.33 pm. Ciliax was almost relieved, for he had been able to get his ships through the worst half of the journey without any major incident. They had been at sea now for nearly fifteen hours.

It was the destroyer *Hermann Schomann* that finally beat off the attack of the British MTBs, when the latter's torpedoes had all missed. This was the first ship-to-ship action.

To the pilots keeping constant watch from above, the British attack was a feeble fiasco. But now they must be on the look-out for the RAF. It was 13.34 hours when the fighters spotted the British aircraft flying low over the wave-tops towards the ships. Ten Spitfires escorting six Swordfish were heading out from the direction of Ramsgate. The Fw.190 and Me.109 pilots immediately attacked and German radio silence was now broken, as the fighter radio controller on board *Scharnhorst* began to give directions to the pilots. Galland at this point issued the order 'Open Visor', which gave the freedom of the wavelengths to his

Under fire from Dover guns

Galland's night fighters escorting ships

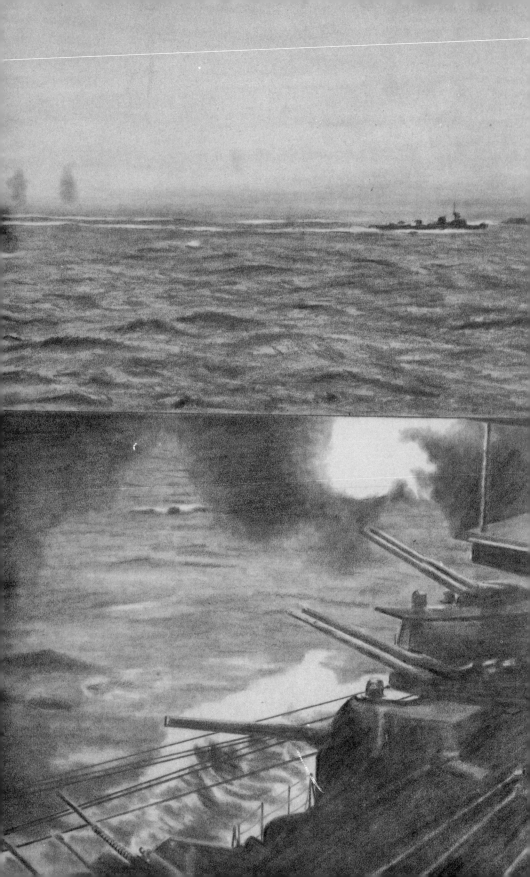

pilots, who could now chatter away at will and allowed them to gain height to attack the enemy. They were no longer tied to low flying, although their main duty was still to guard the ships and avoid being lured away by aerial combat.

With the enemy aircraft about to attack, Galland issued the order for some of his standby pilots to enter the battle, much to the consternation of the Spitfire pilots, who soon found themselves outnumbered and unable adequately to defend the vulnerable Swordfish.

From the bridge of *Scharnhorst*, Ciliax watched through his field glasses, the approaching Swordfish aircraft, with their torpedoes slung under their bellies, getting nearer. They were taking a terrific hammering from Galland's men, yet nothing seemed to stop their onset. To the Luftwaffe pilots it was amazing that these old aircraft flew at all. Their speed must have been only about 80 knots, at most, and with torpedoes slung underneath they were not the easiest aircraft to handle. Time and again Galland's fighters attacked, some pilots lowering their undercarriages and flaps to bring their speed down to that of the enemy. Bullets and cannon shells poured into those six Swordfish, and although the fabric covering was now streaming back from their fuselages in long ribbands, they still staggered on.

As they came into range, the ships' anti-aircraft guns opened fire. The leading aircraft had its lower port wing shot off, but still managed to loose off its torpedo at *Prinz Eugen*. Then it was all over for him as he received a direct hit from one of the guns and crashed into the sea. Nothing the Germans had seen before could compare with the bravery of these Swordfish aircrews. The remaining five aircraft were still making attack approaches, while at the same time Galland's men were pumping shells into them from both sides. The next enemy aircraft came on, then was hit in the main fuel tank by a cannon shell which luckily for its pilot did not explode, though he lost all the fuel from his tank and had to switch to his emergency tank. This gave him only a few minutes flying time, then he was certain to land in the sea. His torpedo splashed into the sea, headed for one of the ships, and once again missed. The aircraft passed over the *Prinz Eugen*, to splash down into the cold waters of the Channel. The next four aircraft

Top: Esmonde's Swordfish crashing into the sea Bottom: Prinz Eugen firing heavy guns as Swordfish attack

suffered similar fates, and of the eighteen men in their aircraft only five survived. They were picked up by the British MTBs.

The Spitfire pilots had witnessed the fate of their friends but had been unable to do much to help. They themselves were taking losses, not so much from the ships' guns as from the Luftwaffe pilots, who outnumbered them about three to one.

There was a lull in the fighting after these attacks. The time now was 14.37 hours, the weather was getting worse. Amazingly, no damage had yet been sustained by the ships. Two of Galland's fighters had been shot down by the Spitfires, but that was all. At his headquarters, Galland himself was in constant touch with the ships. It was difficult for him to form an accurate picture of the fighting, for most of the aerial combat was out of range of the ships. But he knew that the ships had not encountered either enemy ships or aircraft in force. No major warship of the enemy had so far been seen, no large-scale bombing attack by the RAF had yet developed. Hitler had been right; the British were incapable of making quick decisions. Now his audacious plan to sail the ships past Dover in broad daylight was paying off.

The ships were now passing from one command to the other. The Paris Headquarters of Naval Group West were congratulating themselves that all had gone so well for them. Although the journey of the ships was only half over, the worst part had gone without a hitch or mishap. Their worst fears had been groundless, for they had been prepared for a major recovery and salvage exercise had one of the ships been sunk. Now the responsibility was handed over to the Northern Command.

Galland of course still carried his burden of responsibility, and would continue to do so until the ships were safe in home waters. The weather was deteriorating, making it difficult for the enemy to locate the ships and, with the low clouds building up and the constant rain, any bombers that did find them would have to make low level attacks. It was impossible to do high altitude bombing through cloud at this stage in the war, for inventions that were to come into service with the RAF later in the war, were still in the embryo stage.

The enemy continued to send out various small groups of aircraft, which the Luftwaffe pilots soon dealt with. It was the air

'Prinz Eugen' on the Channel dash

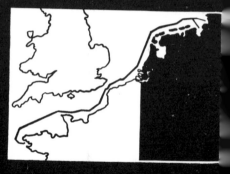

NORTHERN
NAVAL
COMMAND

H.Q. NORTHER
NAVAL COMMA

GALLAND'S
4th SECTOR

GNEISENAU &
PRINZ EUGEN
ARRIVE A.M.
13th

SCHARNHORST HITS
SECOND MINE
22·34 hours

GNEISENAU
24·00 hrs 12th

GNEISENAU HITS
MINE 20·55 hours

JEVER

SCHARN
ARRIVE

GALLAND'S
3rd SECTOR

MAIN BEAUFORT &
HUDSON ATTACK
17·00 hours

O SCHIPHOL

KEY
O GALLANDS HEADQUAR
▽ MARKER BOATS

Scheldt

umbrella that really bore the brunt of the fighting. Although the RAF had not as yet launched a major bombing attack, Galland was prepared, for now the Luftwaffe pilots were operating very close to their own bases. It did not take long to re-arm and re-fuel the fighters when they came in, and the pilots could have a smoke and a brief rest while this was being done. They were keen to be off again, however; they did not waste time unnecessarily.

The ships had now reached Flushing, the time was 15.30 hours. Suddenly disaster of an unseen nature struck *Scharnhorst*. There was a violent underwater explosion that seemed to lift the great ship out of the water. The crew at their various stations were flung about, then there was silence. The great engines had ceased to throb, and all the ship's lighting had gone out. The Luftwaffe Radio Control Room was a shambles, all the radio sets had been shaken loose and lay scattered about. Oberstleutnant Hentschel was suffering from a sprained knee and arm, and control of the fighters from the ship was now impossible. One solitary mine, laid by the RAF, had accomplished what all the bombs and torpedoes had so far failed to do.

From the bridge, Ciliax could see a large oil slick trailing behind the ship. Damage Control reported a large hole in the bottom of the ship on the starboard side, with two compartments flooded.

Meanwhile the rest of the convoy were passing swiftly by, for they had orders to keep going no matter what happened; if disaster struck any of the ships, no other ship was to render assistance, either in picking up survivors or by trying to take the damaged ship in tow.

Ciliax could not estimate how long it would take to repair the *Scharnhorst*, so he ordered Z-29, the leading destroyer, to come alongside and take him and his staff aboard; this of course included the HQ staff of the Fighter Command Afloat. Oberst Ibel sent a signal to Oberstleutnant Dorando aboard the *Prinz Eugen*, explaining the situation, and asked him to take over control of the fighters for the time being.

As the destroyer came alongside, Ciliax and his staff were ready to go, but the swell was so great that it made the transfer from the great ship down to the small destroyer hazardous. Just as the HQ personnel had jumped down onto the rolling, pitching deck of the

G

Top: Z29 in Norwegian waters Bottom: Z38

destroyer, Captain Hoffmann was informed by the Damage
Control party that apart from the hole the mine had made in the
bottom of the ship damage was negligible and the hull compartments had been sealed up. Nine minutes after Ciliax had
transferred himself and his staff across to *Z-29*, *Scharnhorst* was
once again ready to start engines; half an hour after the Admiral's
departure, the great ship was doing 27 knots again, to catch up
with the convoy. The time — 16.05 hours.

Meanwhile, *Z-29* had been spotted by three enemy bombers
who proceeded to attack her. But the Luftwaffe fighters swamped
the British planes, chasing them off before they could do any
damage.

By this time the enemy was stepping up his air attacks, and
Galland sent more of his reserves into battle. Increasingly bad
weather, which was now giving cover to the ships and hindering
the RAF, was also battering Galland's fighter bases in Holland. A
number of pilots made crash landings. The others were so keen to
get back into the battle again, that as soon as their aircraft were
serviced and re-armed, on their own initiative and with no specific
orders to do so, they climbed back into their cockpits and with a
cheerful wave to the ground crews, taxied out and took-off into
the dismal storm clouds. When Galland was told of this enthusiasm
he was agreeably surprised that, after all the misfortunes and
slanders his pilots had suffered this operation should prove such a
morale booster. It is very much to the credit of the Luftwaffe
pilots taking part in this operation that no air attack damaged the
ships. Now, with the weather closing in even more, it was getting
hard for the RAF to find the ships at all. Even flying at sea level,
just above the waves, visibility was no more than one mile.

As the destroyer *Z-29*, with Ciliax and his staff on board, was
ploughing through the waves to catch up with the convoy, her
port engine broke down. This was the second disappointment of
the day for Ciliax, and mishaps usually run in threes. It was not
long before the Admiral got his third. In fact it came only a few
minutes later when he was transferring from *Z-29* to the destroyer
Hermann Schomann. He and his staff were in a cutter going from
one ship to the other when *Scharnhorst* steamed by at 27 knots,
without stopping. Ciliax must have regretted making the decision

to transfer as he saw her vanish into the mist. However, what was done was done, so he climbed aboard *Hermann Schomann* followed by his staff, leaving the destroyer *Z-29* to manage as best she could on one engine.

The next British Naval attack came at about 16.55 hours, when five destroyers approached. These ships had come from Harwich. After a running battle in which they were heavily outnumbered, they were eventually driven off. HMS *Worcester* was set on fire, with damage to her bridge and bows.

The weather by this time had worsened so much that it was difficult for Galland's pilots to distinguish enemy ships from their own. As so often happens in the heat of a battle, some of the pilots attacked their own ships by mistake, as also did some British aircraft. With the cloud base now so low, a pilot breaking momentarily out of the murk would have only one brief glance in which to identify friend from foe. Mistakes were inevitable. The clouds at this point were so full of aircraft of all descriptions, it is surprising that there were no collisions.

The RAF attacks suffered severely from lack of co-ordination, and trying to locate the ships in these weather conditions was like looking for black cats in the dark. Even so, a running battle between enemy aircraft and the Luftwaffe, aided by gunfire from the ships, went on until the hours of darkness. Between 17.00 hours and 19.00 hours the ships were under constant attack by what appeared to be the main enemy force of twin-engined Beaufort torpedo bombers, accompanied by a number of twin-engined Hudsons. Again the enemy had no real chance to press home his attacks, for the barrage put up by the ships was fearsome. The Luftwaffe pilots were doing a good job too, and the sky above the ships was a mass of aircraft in constant battle. Of all the torpedoes the Beauforts dropped, none hit any of the capital ships.

It was just after 19.00 hours and getting dark. Once again the night fighters had joined the ships, and helped the day fighters to turn away the last of the British aircraft. The weary day fighter pilots, who had borne the brunt of the battle, returned to the nearest bases in Holland for rest and sleep leaving the night fighters to stay with the ships. Tomorrow was another day. They

Handley Page Hampden

had served their Fuehrer well and Galland was proud of them. He sent out messages of congratulations to all aircrews taking part in the day's operation. Now it was up to the ships themselves.

On board the ships, the effects of the day's battle were being cleared up. Now that darkness had descended, the crews could relax a little, stepping down in rotation from action stations for food and a brief rest. *Scharnhorst* had by this time caught up with the rest of the squadron. The ships were just level with Amsterdam. There was comparative quiet once again on board, with only the familiar, almost friendly wind howling and the waves lashing against the steel plates. With the worst three-quarters of the journey behind them, Ciliax's men could look forward hopefully to a quiet run into Brunsbuttel at the mouth of the Kiel Canal. But war bristles with the unpredictable. As *Gneisenau* was sailing level with the Friesian Islands she struck a mine laid by an RAF aircraft only an hour before. There was a great flash, and the battlecruiser could be plainly seen from the other ships, illuminated by the glare. Captain Fein ordered the damage-repair parties to work at once, and the engines were stopped to prevent an excessive intake of water below decks. The damage was only slight, however, and the repair teams soon had it sufficiently under control for the ship to proceed on her way. Only half an hour's delay was recorded, which stands to the credit of her Damage Control parties.

One and a half hours later, at 22.34, *Scharnhorst* struck her second mine, also dropped by the RAF. This time the damage was severe. The starboard main engine was out of action, while the other two main engines were stopped, their propeller shafts jammed by the explosion. The damage repair teams worked feverishly, reporting back to Captain Hoffmann that the ship was flooding badly in several compartments. These were sealed off, but not before *Scharnhorst* had developed a seven-degree list to starboard. With the damage to the engines, and extensive damage in the dynamo room, communications aboard broke down. Lights had gone out, leaving the ship drifting in complete darkness towards the Friesian Islands.

It says much for *Scharnhorst*'s engineers that after an hour and a quarter Captain Hoffmann was told that the ship was once again ready to proceed at a slow rate of knots, running on the starboard and centre engines, while the shaft on the port engine, the one furthest away from the blast, was still jammed. Gradually, the ship came to life, the two engines allowed her to proceed at 10 knots to start with; then she was able to work up to 15 knots.

The *Prinz Eugen* and the crippled *Gneisenau* had by this time reached the mouth of the Elbe. When they asked for the assistance of pilots to help them berth, they found that none would be available until first light of dawn. Naval Command North had made no arrangements for their arrival. The ships waited in the Elbe estuary for dawn.

Scharnhorst meanwhile was making slow progress towards Wilhelmshaven, where she arrived at 10.30 am. An hour previously at 9.30, Admiral Ciliax and his staff returned to his flagship. So, in the early hours of the 13th of February 1942, ended the worst part of the ships' journey.

Later that same day, the 13th, the German High Command issued a terse statement to the effect that during the battle of the previous day, the Brest Squadron under the command of Vice Admiral Ciliax had transferred safely from Brest to ports in Germany, travelling up the English Channel with the loss of only one E-boat and seventeen aircraft. The British on the other hand had lost forty-nine aircraft, and one destroyer had been hit and set on fire. It went on to mention that the Luftwaffe pilots under the command of General Galland and General Coeler (Bomber and Reconnaissance Commander) had distinguished themselves during the day's fighting.

It seems on the face of it a surprisingly reserved statement, considering the great moral victory that had been achieved over the British, but the German High Command knew that Operation 'Thunderbolt', which would only be ended when the ships entered Norwegian waters, was not yet over. This in their eyes was only the end of the first stage of the transfer of the ships. Nevertheless, there was much rejoicing in Germany when the news of the 'Channel Dash' was released to the public. The only man in Germany who could not celebrate the victory was Grand Admiral Raeder. In his eyes the whole operation was a disaster. The use of ships that could have been doing important work on the high seas

Gneisenau

against the enemy in a purely defensive role, was entirely contrary to his principles.

In fact the second phase of 'Thunderbolt' could not properly be implemented. Both *Gneisenau* and *Scharnhorst* went into dry dock for repair, while *Prinz Eugen* sailed, accompanied by the pocket battleship *Admiral Scheer*, for Norwegian waters. Once again Galland's pilots put up an air umbrella, while Galland himself set up his headquarters at Jever, just outside Wilhelmshaven, later transferring to Esbjerg in Denmark, and then finally to Stavangar in Norway.

The RAF carried out massive bombing attacks on both *Scharnhorst* and *Gneisenau* two weeks later. For three nights, between February 25th and 27th both ships received the attention of Bomber Command. It was *Gneisenau* that suffered all the damage, while *Scharnhorst* escaped unscathed. Damage to *Gneisenau's* bows and foredeck was so serious that it was decided not to refit her. Instead she was towed to the port of Gydnia in Poland where her hulk was filled with concrete and she was used as a Blockship fort. Six months after the raid *Scharnhorst* was once again ready for sea, when she continued her tour of duty in Norwegian waters as Hitler had originally ordered. *Prinz Eugen*, already working in Norwegian waters, was hit by a torpedo from the British submarine H.M.S. *Trident* which blew her stern off: this was only twelve days after leaving Brest and, although she managed to limp into Aasfiord and anchor, she never recovered from this attack nor was she used again at sea. After the war the Americans used her at Bikini Atol where she was sunk in one of the atomic tests.

Scharnhorst's life ended in a great battle in Arctic waters, where she was intercepted by ships of the British Home Fleet and sunk on Boxing Day, 1943.

Adolf Galland

Born in the town of Westerholt in Westphalia on March 19th, 1912, Adolf Galland was one of four brothers. They were the children of an old established Westphalian family, their forefathers having settled there in about 1742. Adolf's father was bailiff to

Showing 'Gneisenau' at Kiel after the dash

Count von Westerholt, a post the family had held for nearly a hundred and eighty years.

After attending elementary school in Westerholt, young Adolf went to finish his education at Buer. It was while he was here that he became interested in flying, for there was a great vogue in Germany in those days for amateur gliding. At the age of seventeen, with his father's permission, he joined a gliding club and made his first flight. He found it difficult to master the art, but even so it was not long before he was earning a name for himself with long distance endurance flights. He enjoyed flying and made his mind up that, when he reached the right age, he would apply to become an airline pilot with Lufthansa.

At the age of twenty he matriculated, and by this time he had passed his gliding instructor's examination. Soon he owned his own glider. The time was now right for him to apply for the entrance examination papers to become a Lufthansa pupil pilot. He was overjoyed when, along with nineteen others out of the twenty thousand who sat for the entrance exam, he was told he had been accepted. So with the blessing of his parents, he went into the German Civil Flying Training School. On completion of his course, he was soon flying regular civil airline flights.

The year was 1934. Already Germany was secretly preparing for war under her new leader Adolf Hitler. It was a time when pilots were in great demand for the new German Air Force — the Luftwaffe. Galland, on hearing of the need for fighter pilots, applied to become one. He was accepted and went to Italy for training. On return he was posted to the Schleissheim Flying School. A Lieutenant now, he became an instructor at the Schleissheim Military Flying Training School.

When Spain was caught up in a civil war, Nazi Germany offered the help of her air force and army to Franco's rebels. Among those to volunteer for active service was Galland, and he joined the German Kondor Legion in 1936. Thanks largely to the men and machines provided by Nazi Germany and Fascist Italy, the Insurgents won, overthrowing the Republican Government. The war in Spain taught the German units much. They were able to try out their new machines, both tanks and aircraft, under actual combat conditions; that was to prove useful to them when

Adolf Galland and his mechanic

hostilities started in Europe, although opposition in the air was negligible. To Galland and his companions it was a proving ground for tactics as well as machines. They learnt the importance of ground attack and close support, and gained much confidence during the months of aerial combat. German bombers became adept at the destruction of undefended towns like the Basque capital Guermica. When the war ended, Galland was no 'ace', but he had flown over three hundred sorties during the war. When the victorious Kondor Legion returned home, Galland found he had been awarded the Spanish 'Cross of Gold' — with Diamonds. Only fourteen of these were awarded after the campaign, so it was a great honour.

On October 1st, 1939, Galland was promoted to the rank of Hauptmann (or Major). He was 27 and already engaged in the Polish campaign, flying seventy sorties in twenty-seven days.

When Hitler declared war on Europe, the methods used by the Luftwaffe to pave the way for the advancing soldiers was very successful. It was not long before Germany had under her control most of her neighbouring countries. Britain had declared war soon after German troops moved into Warsaw, and with the fall of France, found that only a small Channel of water separated the two opposing forces.

Galland found himself serving in France in 1940, and on May 10th shot down his first British aircraft, an RAF Hurricane. On July 10th, he was awarded the 'Knights Cross' and promoted. Later that same year, on December 25th, he was again decorated, this time with the Oak Leaves to the Knight's Cross in honour of his fortieth air victory. Many adventures came his way, and he himself was shot down and wounded on more than one occasion. He was a colourful character and the German press made great use of him; with his many exploits he became a popular hero. Promotion and decorations were heaped on him, and he deserved both. When he was given his own Staffel or Squadron to command, he was promoted to the rank of Oberstleutnant or Wing Commander. It was not long before he was promoted again, to command a Geschwader or Group with the courtesy title of Kommodore. His Geschwader was located in the Pas de Calais area, one of the only two left in France when Hitler ordered the opening of his offensive against the Russians.

By this time his score as a fighter pilot had crept up into the nineties, and after his ninety-fourth air victory he received the 'Diamonds' to his 'Oak Leaves with Sabres'. The end of 1941 his official score stood at ninety-six, but as he himself was loath to claim any further aircraft shot down — in case he might be banned from combat flying — there is little doubt that he had scored a few more unclaimed victories.

With the tragic death of Molders, Galland was appointed to fill his post as 'Inspector-General of the Fighter Arm'. His was a popular appointment, for he had earned the respect of everyone. Unfortunately for Galland, he was forbidden to fly further combat missions, something he had dreaded. Still, he had not been banned from flying, and that was something.

On June 18th, 1942, he was again promoted, this time to the rank of Oberst (Group Captain). The end of 1942 saw him as a Generalleutnant (Air Vice Marshal), this made him the youngest General in the German Armed Forces, at the age of 30. His job as commander of the fighter section of the Luftwaffe in Europe was not one to be envied; he soon came into direct conflict with Göring, mainly because he was not the type of person to bury his head in the sand, nor would he tell the Chief of the Luftwaffe only what he wanted to hear. Instead of joining the little group of sycophants surrounding Göring, as he had been invited to do, he chose to remain with his fighter pilots. At this time in the war, the balance of power was with the Allies. Galland continually warned Göring of this fact, but the Chief of the Luftwaffe refused to listen. Gradually a strong enmity grew up between the two. It was brought to a head when Galland was refused the use of the new and revolutionary Messerschmitt fighter, the Me 262, powered by jet engines, as a fighter plane, the job it had been intended for. The Allies had nothing to compete with the 262. This was when Galland realised how weak was Göring's relationship with Hitler, for his Chief either could not or would not stand up against the Fuehrer's insane insistence that bomber aircraft were all he needed to combat the Allies in the air. So the Me.262 went into production as a bomber, not a fighter.

Time was getting short for the Luftwaffe. With the heavy

bombing of strategic targets, by the Allies and the advance of the Russians, things began to look decidedly unhealthy for the Germans. The situation was bitterly frustrating to Galland, who had his own ideas on essential measures to be taken. He wanted to augment his fighter squadrons with the Me.262s, but he could not get his way. At the end of December 1944 Göring sent for him and told him to go on indefinite leave: he had been relieved of his post.

This was the last straw for the fighter pilots under Galland. They had been under great pressure from the Allies for many months now, and all the thanks they got from their leaders were rebukes for not halting the heavy bombing. They had never really been forgiven for losing the Battle of Britain; now they had lost the only man they had ever respected as a leader, the only man, they felt, who could do something to help Germany. The situation became ugly and, when Göring heard that his fighter pilots were near revolt because of the action he had taken over Galland, he decided to form a special Staffel of 16 Me.262s and put Galland in command. The object of the Staffel was supposed to be to prove the aircraft as a fighter — and with a bit of luck, perhaps, remove Galland from this world. It did succeed in stopping an uprising in the fighter arm, although by this time it was too late to make any difference to the outcome of the war.

Galland and his staffel had many adventures, but ultimately the odds were too great. In 1945, when the Allies overran Germany, Galland was taken prisoner of war. He is alive today, having proved himself a competent leader with plenty of courage, uncompromising in standing by his beliefs and unshakeable in shouldering his responsibilities.

Aftermath

Every story has two sides, and this one is no exception. For the British the 'Channel Dash' is a sad and too familiar tale of inadequate resources and mismanagement, and the bad luck and misfortune which so often attends such failings. The British had not anticipated that Hitler's famous intuition would send his powerful raiding squadron dashing east. The naval staffs on both sides thought alike. The British Admiralty expected what Admiral Raeder wanted — a breakout to the west, with the two battle-cruisers resuming their already successful activities in the Atlantic.

At the beginning of 1941, the *Scharnhorst* and *Gneisenau* had left the German port of Kiel. They sailed through the Denmark Straits and out into the Atlantic, dodging the British Home Fleet based at Scapa Flow. Britain depended on supplies brought in by her own and Allied merchant shipping for survival; during the next two months, the two great German battleships roamed the Atlantic shipping lanes, sinking over 100,000 tons of Allied shipping.

It was on the 22nd of March, 1941, at 07.00 hours, that the two great ships put into the French port of Brest for repairs. France had been under German rule for nearly a year by this time, but the French dockyard workers were unwilling co-operators with their conquerors. So the Germans had transferred some of their own workers from Wilhelmshaven, and these were the only personnel allowed to work on the German battleships. They assessed the damage to the ships and notified their Captains. *Scharnhorst's* repairs would take at least ten weeks, for she had developed serious defects in her boilers. *Gneisenau* was more fortunate, needing only minor repairs. She would soon be at sea again.

After the heavy sinkings of Allied ships by the two raiders, the British had been hunting them on the High Seas unsuccessfully and were temporarily relieved when both vessels docked in Brest. Now they could attack them as sitting targets. Night and day the RAF visited Brest, plastering the harbour with bombs.

One of the most daring attacks made by the RAF was the lone attack on April 6th 1941 by Flying Officer Kenneth Campbell, piloting an RAF Coastal Command Beaufort torpedo bomber of 22 Squadron, stationed at St Eval in Cornwall.

Diving through the clouds, Campbell saw the *Gneisenau* berthed alongside a wall at the north end of the harbour. She was heavily protected by anti-aircraft guns, and the natural surroundings of the harbour. Any low-flying aircraft would almost certainly be committing suicide in attempting an attack; should the pilot manage to get through the barrage put up by the guns, he would then surely

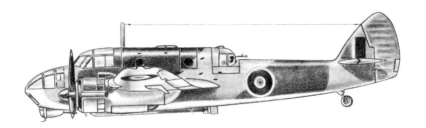

Bristol Beaufort I

Left
F/O Campbell

crash into the high ground surrounding the harbour. Disregarding all these odds, Campbell dived in to attack. Flying low over the water, he released his torpedo. But the ack-ack gunners found their target, sending the lone Beaufort crashing into the sea, a flaming mass. His torpedo hit *Gneisenau* in the stern on the starboard side, blowing a great hole through which tons of water rushed. A salvage tug had the greatest difficulty in keeping *Gneisenau* afloat.

The bodies of the RAF crew were rescued from the harbour and placed on the *Gneisenauu's* quarterdeck, where they were draped in flags and a guard of honour was mounted as a mark of respect. This gallant aircrew had captured the admiration of the French who saw the attack, and the respect of the Germans who had suffered it. It was a report sent by the French Resistance to the British which afterwards secured the award of a posthumous VC for Flying Officer Campbell. The Official Citation reads as follows.

Awards
Victoria Cross

The King has been graciously pleased to confer the Victoria Cross on the undermentioned officer in recognition of most conspicuous bravery :-

F/O K. CAMPBELL, RAFVR (deceased), No.22 Sqn. — This officer was the pilot of a Beaufort aircraft of Coastal Command which was detailed to attack an enemy battle cruiser in Brest Harbour at first light on the morning of April 6th, 1941. The aircraft did not return, but it is now known that a torpedo attack was carried out with the utmost daring.

The battle cruiser was secured alongside the wall on the north shore of the harbour, protected by a stone mole bending round it from the west. On rising ground behind the ship stood protective batteries of guns. Other batteries were clustered thickly round the two arms of land which encircle the outer harbour. In this outer harbour near the mole were moored three heavily armed anti-aircraft ships, guarding the battle cruiser. Even if an aircraft succeeded in penetrating these formidable defences, it would be almost impossible, after delivering a low-level attack, to avoid crashing into the rising ground beyond.

This was well known to F/O Campbell who, despising the heavy odds, went cheerfully and resolutely to the task. He ran the gauntlet of the defences. Coming in almost at sea level, he passed the anti-aircraft ships at less than mast-height in the very mouths of their guns, and skimming over the mole launched a torpedo at point-blank range. The battle cruiser was severely damaged below the water-line and was obliged to return to the dock whence she had come only the day before.

By pressing home his attack at close quarters in the face of a withering fire on a course fraught with extreme peril, F/O Campbell displayed valour of the highest order.

To show their respect for his bravery and that of his crew, the Germans gave them a funeral with full military honours.

The damage caused by Campbell's torpedo put *Gneisenau* in dry dock for repairs for six months, which meant that she would be out of action twice as long as *Scharnhorst*. Had two torpedoes found their target, instead of just one, there is little doubt that the *Gneisenau* would have sunk. As German Naval HQ heard the news of the lone British attacker, and the damage he had done, a decision was made to use the ships for training purposes. On June 1st, *Prinz Eugen* joined *Scharnhorst* and *Gneisenau* in Brest harbour. She had just returned from doing battle with the Royal Navy, after a tour with the *Bismarck* which had been successful until *Bismarck* was sunk.

Brest was now becoming a popular place with the RAF, both during the day and at night. The constant damage caused by the raids, and the severe loss of personnel, decided the Germans to barrack the crews of the ships in a camp a few miles outside the town.

The British, realising the Germans might now decide to transfer their ships to safer home waters, established three separate forms of surveillance. Submarines were stationed outside Brest harbour, Coastal Command of the RAF carried out dusk to dawn patrols in Hudson aircraft fitted with air-to-sea search radar, while radar stations along the British coast kept a constant lookout. On top of this RAF Fighter Command made constant daylight Channel sweeps. The British thus effectively covered all likely means of escape from Brest harbour open to the German ships.

The Air Ministry prepared its three commands (Bomber, Fighter and Coastal) in a letter issued on April 29th 1941, to be ready for a break-out by the German ships attempting to reach the safety of home waters, stating that the most likely route for them to take was the Channel route. They also stated that it would – in their opinion – be unlikely that the Germans would sail through the Straits of Dover in broad daylight. Should this happen, however, they felt a unique opportunity would be afforded to the RAF to attack the ships. With this in mind the forces of Bomber Command were ordered to have a suitable number of aircraft standing by. The date suggested by the Air Ministry as likely for a break-out by the Germans was between April 30th–May 4th 1941.

The Air Ministry by issuing this letter showed their initiative. They may not have got their dates right, but they were thinking on the right lines. In fact they were thinking in advance of the Germans themselves, for it was not until a month after the Air Ministry letter was issued that the Germans began to consider looking at the Channel route seriously. Perhaps knowledge of the letter itself had set them thinking.

The RAF continued to bomb Brest, returning after each operation with reconnaissance photos. It was during December that the photographs showed the movement of the ships from dry dock. In spite of the constant raids, repair work was completed and now the ships were once again almost seaworthy. The information was passed on to the Admiralty by the RAF, who promptly dispatched seven submarines to form what they termed an 'iron ring' outside Brest harbour. However, due to heavy submarine losses, the iron ring was not allowed to remain in position for long. By January 2nd 1942, the RAF were once again the only service keeping a constant watch on the ships. Reports by both Fighter and Coastal Commands told of the continuous movement of German ships in the Channel. Aerial reconnaissance photographs showed minesweeping activities and a general concentration of German destroyers towards Brest. Great acitivity was also spotted among the E-boats along the French coast. Was all this a red herring operation to cover a break-out to the west, or were the Germans really getting ready for the movement up Channel of their Brest Squadron? Once again the Admiralty decided to station submarines outside Brest harbour, but could only spare two, *H-50* and *H-34*. The submarines took up their stations on January 29th, with orders to patrol the 'most likely escape route'. On January 31st *H-34* broke down and returned to Falmouth, being replaced on February 1st by *H-43*.

The British could not afford to take a chance, so on the 3rd of February 1942 Operation 'Fuller' was born. The object of this operation was to prevent the German ships reaching home waters by sinking them if possible. Ruefully the British took stock of the forces at their disposal. There was no capital ship available to take on the German ships in southern waters at the time, for the Home Fleet was up in Scapa Flow. Neither did the British Admiralty have any intention of transferring it south. The most formidable weapons the British had were torpedo bombers and motor torpedo boats. At St Eval in Cornwall, Nos.86 and 217 RAF Squadrons had a total of twelve Beaufort torpedo-carrying aircraft, while seven more Beauforts of 217 were at Thorney Island near Portsmouth. The only other Beaufort squadron available was No.42, stationed at Leuchars up in Scotland, which had fourteen aircraft and could be moved down to Coltishall on the east coast. These torpedo-carrying aircraft, a total of thirty-three, were all that RAF Coastal Command could spare for Operation 'Fuller'. It was to Bomber Command of the RAF, that the Service Chiefs turned hopefully, should all else fail. To this end 300 bomber aircraft were put on immediate standby.

These aircraft included *Sterlings, Halifaxes, Wellingtons, Blenheims* and *Hampdens*, the *Hampdens* being also fitted out for minelaying.

The Royal Navy was not in much better shape, for the only means they had of deliverying an attack on the German ships, was with torpedo-carrying Swordfish, motor torpedo boats and destroyers. Only six Swordfish were available. These belonged to the famous 825 Squadron, which had lost most of its aircraft when the carrier *Ark Royal* had been sunk, and which was in the process of being re-formed at Lee-on-Solent. The commander of the half-formed squadron was Lieutenant Commander Eugene Esmond, who had already done battle in Swordfish aircraft against the *Bismarck*. For the most part, though, the British Navy would have to rely on six twenty-year-old destroyers stationed at Sheerness, in the Thames estuary. There were also eight motor torpedo boats on the Kentish coast, five at Dover, and three more at Ramsgate. The British Admiralty decided to move two of their units, the six Swordfish from Lee-on-Solent to Manston, and the six destroyers from Sheerness to Harwich. These then were the main British forces available to stop the possible German Channel dash, although the RAF were prepared to throw into the battle a total of 300 bombers a few of which were minelaying Hampden aircraft.

In the minds of the British Chiefs of Staff one thing was sure, if the Germans did move their ships up-Channel, they would want to go through the narrowest point during the hours of darkness. 'Never underestimate your enemy', had always been a British maxim, but on this occasion they were to do exactly that.

Two other factors in the British defences were the coastal guns at Dover and the radar stations along the South Coast. The Dover gun installations were unfortunately not by any means complete at this time, but nevertheless, under the command of the British army, they were a formidable arm of defence. The radar installations were also undergoing alterations at the time, some of the older sets being in process of replacement by later models.

Just before the inauguration of Operation 'Fuller', steps were taken to set up an early warning system. To this end the Admiralty sent two submarines to Brest, to carry out dog-leg patrols, outside Brest Harbour. Costal Command of the RAF set up three patrols of Hudson aircraft, fitted with sea scanning radar. The most southern one was to patrol a dog-leg similar to that of the patrolling submarine. This patrol was code-named 'Stopper'. The middle patrol covered a line from Ushant almost to Jersey, and was code-named 'Line SE'. The third and last Hudson patrol covered the channel from Le Havre to Boulogne, code-named 'Habo'. These patrols interlinked, forming one great search area,

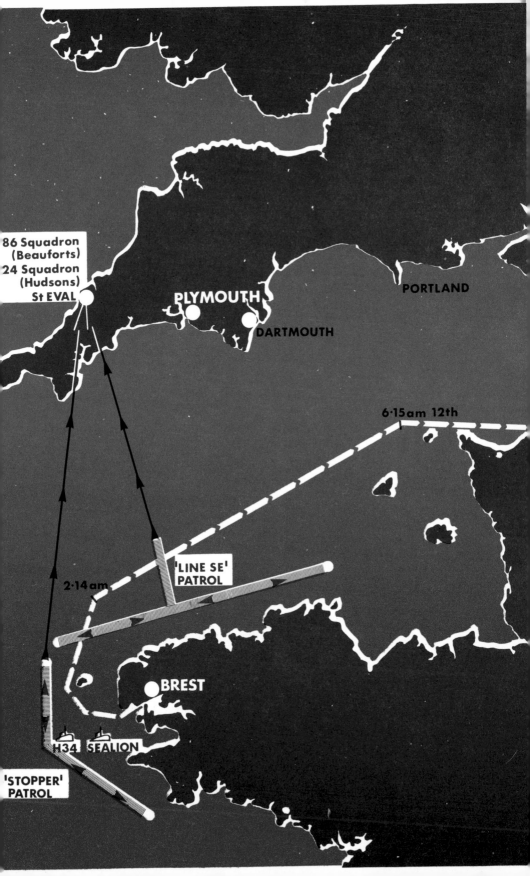

86 Squadron
(Beauforts)
24 Squadron
(Hudsons)
St EVAL

PLYMOUTH

PORTLAND

DARTMOUTH

6·15am 12th

'LINE SE'
PATROL

2·14am

BREST

H34   SEALION

'STOPPER'
PATROL

with the patrolling aircraft sweeping a regular pattern. This was a reasonably tight net, backed up by reconnaissance photographs of Brest harbour.

One final gesture by the Admiralty was to dispatch another submarine, HMS *Sealion*, from Portsmouth to join the other two patrolling off Brest. *Sealion's* captain had instructions to stay close to the harbour. The date was now February 9th, 1942.

The Group in Fighter Command responsible for providing bombers' fighter escort was No.11 Group (Southern Command) with its Headquarters at Uxbridge. They had fighter wings stationed at Hornchurch, Debden, Kenley, Biggin Hill, Tangmere, Hawkinge, North Weald, Hendon, Duxford and Northolt.

The British chain of command at the time was as follows:

NAVAL —   First Sea Lord — Sir Dudley Pound
           Assistant Chief of Staff (Home Operations) — Rear Admiral Power
           Commander-in-Chief, Dover — Vice Admiral Bertram Ramsey
           Flag Officer Commanding Submarines — Admiral Sir Max Horton
           Commander 21st Destroyer Flotilla — Captain Mark Pizey
           Commander MTBs — Dover — Lieutenant Commander Nigel Pumphrey
           Commander 825 Squadron — Lieutenant Commander Eugene Esmond
RAF —   AOC Coastal Command — Air Chief Marshal Sir Philip Joubert
           AOC No.11 Group — Air Vice Marshal Trafford Leigh-Mallory
           RAF Liaison Officer to Admiral Ramsey — Wing Commander Bobby Constable-Roberts
           Senior Controller Radar, Fighter Command — Wing Commander M. Jarvis
           Station Commander, Manston — Wing Commander Tom Gleave
           Station Commander, Kenley — Group Captain Victor Beamish

RAF raid on Brest

RAF Controller, Biggin Hill — Squadron Leader Bill
Igoe

RAF Controller, Swingate — Flight Lieutenant Gerald
Kidd

The whole 'Fuller' scheme was geared for a break-out by the
German ships to pass through the Straits of Dover during the
night.

After the air-raid that held the ships up in Brest for those vital
two hours on February 11th, British Intelligence did not register
any signs of the reconnaissance photographs betraying the
imminent departure of the ships.

When the ships finally did clear port, they should have been
seen by the submarine HMS *Sealion*, which should have been
patrolling outside the harbour of Brest. But this submarine was
not on station, as her captain, Lieutenant Commander G.R. Colvin
had put out to sea to recharge his batteries. No replacement was
sent. Of the other two submarines, one patrolling to the south of
Brest stood no chance of seeing the ships, and the third submarine,
which should have made contact, was unfortunately at the
furthest end of its patrol when the ships sailed through. The
Germans could not of course know this. They had not planned the
two hour delay.

Good fortune persisted for the Germans, and it seems as if fate
was indeed looking after them. The ships sailed unnoticed through
the area Coastal Command was supposed to be patrolling. At this
stage in the war, airborne radar was in its infancy. The sets carried
by the aircraft were air-to-sea search radar, and not always
efficient. They were the early ASV Mark II sets, with a scanning
range of about thirty miles.

On the evening of 11th February 1942, the first aircraft left
St Eval to patrol the 'stopper' stretch at 6.27 pm, for these were
dusk to dawn patrols. The captain of this aircraft was Flight-
Lieutenant C.L. Wilson of 224 Squadron. Although the stars were
shining in the sky, there was no moon out. Searching at night
without a moon is visually impossible, so it had to be done
entirely with radar. Just after 7.15 pm, the aircraft was flying at a
thousand feet near Ushant when it almost collided with a German
JU-88 night fighter. The radar operator on the Hudson hastily

Lockheed 'Hudson'

switched off his set, but when he tried to switch it on again after evasive action had been taken there was no response. Twenty-two minutes later, Wilson decided to return to base as search operations without radar were impossible. At base the trouble was found to be nothing more serious than a blown fuse – but not until over forty minutes had been spent by the radar technicians trying to trace the fault. Wilson was allocated another aircraft, but here again fate was on the side of the Germans, for this aircraft suffered from damp plugs, and refused to start. Almost another hour went by before the engines spluttered into life. Meanwhile a third Hudson was hastily sent to take over the 'Stopper' patrol. This aircraft, commanded by Squadron Leader G. Bartlett, was trouble free, and had its radar set functioning correctly, but by that time the Germans had sailed through the 'Stopper' patrol area undetected.

The fate of the aircraft on 'Line SE' was very similar to Wilson's. This aircraft was commanded by Flight Lieutenant G.S. Bennett, who took off twenty minutes after Wilson. On take-off his radar set had been fully operational, but on arrival over the search area his radar operator found the set to be unserviceable. For over an hour and a half he patrolled, hoping the radar operator could get the set operating again, but fate would not allow it. Finally in despair Bennett broke radio silence, explained the situation to base, and was ordered to return. The time was now 9.15 pm, but this time no replacement aircraft was sent out to take over from Bennett, and another gap was open for the Germans to sail through.

The final patrol, 'Habo', covering the area from Le Havre to Boulogne came under 223 squadron, the sister squadron to 224 stationed at Thorney Island, this patrol started just after midnight and was supposed to finish at 7.15 am. Two aircraft patrolled this route. The first, commanded by Sergeant Smith, left Thorney Island at 12.32 am and stayed on patrol until 5.54 am. Nothing unusual was sighted. The second aircraft, commanded by Flying Officer Alexander, took-off at 3.55 am, being due to return at 7.15 am. This meant that for a period two aircraft were searching in the 'Habo' patrol area. Fate again intervened, this time in the form of fog in the Channel. So dense did it become that an hour before Alexander was due back, the controller at Thorney Island recalled his aircraft fearing the fog would prevent him from landing at his appointed hour. Had he remained on patrol during that vital hour, his radar operator would surely have seen the ships on his screen. So fate was kind to the Germans, clearing gaps in the British early warning screen wide enough to sail an armada through. No wonder Ciliax marvelled at his luck as he spent a peaceful night sailing the dangerous waters.

The next phase of the journey, should have been covered by radar stations set up along the south coast. At this time the British were using old 'M' sets. These were the sets Martini had tuned into for jamming purposes. Here again confusion reigned, for these old 'M' sets were in the process of being replaced by new 'K' sets. So far the Germans did not know about the 'K' sets, neither did Martini know the frequency they operated on. When Martini started up his jamming of the British sets, therefore, he was only interfering with the transmissions of the old 'M' sets. The 'K' sets were still fully operational. At a radar station on top of Beachy Head, equipped with both types of sets, strange things were happening.

The old 'M' set was misbehaving, while the new 'K' set showed clearly movement in the channel. The combination of circling aircraft and fast moving ships (the ships' speed at this point was about 30 knots), confused the radar operators. Their job was to look for ships, and as the normal traffic did not travel the Channel at that speed, they could not make head or tail of what the plot on their radar screens meant. So they notified both the RAF and the Navy. Neither service was much interested, both believing the German ships to be still in Brest, and still feeling secure in their minds that the early warning screen of submarines and *Hudson* aircraft would have given an earlier warning should the ships have left port after the air raid. It is an error closely reminiscent of the complete disregard of radar warning by the American authorities before the Japanese attack on Pearl Harbour.

General Martini and his men were doing a first-class job. Not only had he set up jamming stations along the French coast, but he had also equipped two Heinkel III aircraft with special jamming equipment. These aircraft took off at dawn on February 12th and flew in advance of the fighters guarding the ships. There is no doubt about the success of Martini's work.

By this time, however, the British were getting radar reports from several airfields of what could only be assumed to be aircraft circling over fast moving ships. These reports were coming from airfields equipped with 'K' sets. Still nobody seemed very concerned. The time was 8.30 am, and although the ships with Galland's escorting aircraft had been discovered, nobody believed it could be happening.

At 9.0 am, two things happened. First, General Martini's coastal radar jamming stations opened up, the previous jamming having been done by his two Heinkel aircraft. Second, the Beaufort torpedo bombers of No.42 Squadron, which were stationed up in Scotland at Leuchars took-off for Coltishall in East Anglia.

The time was now 10.0 am. Still no action had been taken to check on the radar reports, although when Squadron Leader Bill Igoe, the Controller at Biggin Hill came on duty at 8.0 am, he noted the plots on the radar and came to the correct conclusion. When he rang 11 Group and informed them he thought operation 'Fuller' should be activated, nobody seemed to know what he was talking about. Disappointed, Igoe rang through to his old friend Squadron Leader Oxspring of 91 squadron at Hawkinge. Explaining the situation to him, he asked him to fly a sortie and find out if his theory was correct. Oxspring agreed, and took with him Sergeant Beaumont in a second Spitfire. By the time these two aircraft got into the air the time was 10.10 am. At 10.40 am fifteen miles off Le Touquet, Oxspring and Beaumont encountered the German ships and their fighter escort. As soon as Galland's pilots saw them they raced into attack, but the two Spitfires climbed smartly into the clouds to evade the German fighters. They had seen all they needed to confirm Bill Igoe's fears.

All British and Allied pilots had strict instructions to maintain radio silence over the Channel — except in an emergency. This to Squadron Leader Oxspring was an emergency. Although he was unaware of code name 'Fuller', he radio'd back to base that he and Beaumont had just seen three German capital ships surrounded by an escort of twenty-plus destroyers and MTBs sailing up Channel, heading for the Straits of Dover. This was the first official notice the British had that the ships had left Brest.

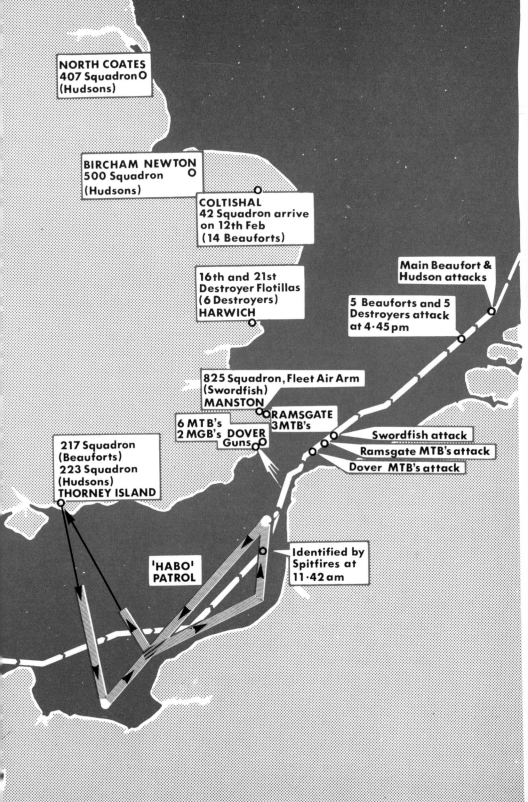

NORTH COATES
407 Squadron O
(Hudsons)

BIRCHAM NEWTON
500 Squadron O
(Hudsons)

COLTISHAL
42 Squadron arrive
on 12th Feb
(14 Beauforts)

Main Beaufort &
Hudson attacks

16th and 21st
Destroyer Flotillas
(6 Destroyers)
HARWICH

5 Beauforts and 5
Destroyers attack
at 4·45 pm

825 Squadron, Fleet Air Arm
(Swordfish)
MANSTON

RAMSGATE
3 MTB's

6 MTB's
2 MGB's DOVER
Guns

Swordfish attack

Ramsgate MTB's attack

Dover MTB's attack

217 Squadron
(Beauforts)
223 Squadron
(Hudsons)
THORNEY ISLAND

'HABO'
PATROL

Identified by
Spitfires at
11·42 am

The Germans also heard his radio transmission, and notified Galland at his headquarters. Galland at this point faced the decision of issuing the order 'Open Visor' or maintaining radio silence. Wisely he decided on the latter, for it would be over another hour yet before his men would meet and do battle with the enemy.

· When the British received Oxspring's radio call, the reaction time was appallingly long. One must remember however, that the whole of operation 'Fuller' was geared to a night dash through the Straits. All personnel on standby were at rest or even off duty, only coming on in the evening. The British themselves couldn't understand how the ships had slipped through such an elaborate early warning system. They literally were caught napping.

Two other Spitfires were seen over the ships at the same time by Oxspring and Beaumont. These were Group Captain Beamish and Wing-Commander Boyd's aircraft from Kenley. These two officers had taken it upon themselves to fly a Channel sweep, just to keep the war going, and let the Germans know that not all Spitfires were grounded because of the bad weather. This was fine, until they came slap across the German ships on their return flight. They did not think to break radio silence however and warn Dover to expect the ships in the sights of their shore batteries in a short while. They kept radio silence, and only when they were being de-briefed by the station's Intelligence Officer did their story come out.

As soon as Oxspring landed, Bill Igoe was on the phone to him, and they both decided the wisest move was for Bill to make contact with the Air Officer Commanding Number Eleven Group, Air Vice-Marshal Trafford Leigh-Mallory. This was to prove difficult however, for Leigh-Mallory was at Northolt reviewing units of the Belgian Air Force under his command, and when Bill Igoe phoned through to 11 Group he was informed that the AOC could not be disturbed.

At 11.35 am the AOC eventually came to the telephone. It was Beamish he spoke to, as Bill Igoe had given up trying by this time. At last the vital information had reached the right ears, and things started happening.

By this time the Navy was also beginning to get reports of the

Supermarine 'Spitfire'

breakout of the ships, and the Admiralty notified Admiral Ramsey at Dover that the German ships would soon be sailing past his Headquarters at Dover Castle. From the Castle, with its fine view overlooking Dover harbour and the Channel, Ramsey directed all Channel Operations. The RAF Liaison Officer attached to Admiral Ramsey's Staff was Wing-Commander 'Bobby' Constable-Roberts. He was the first officer to take official action against the Germans. He contacted No.16 Group of Coastal Command and asked them to transfer the Beauforts of 86 Squadron from St Eval in Cornwall to Manston in Kent. Also he suggested that the Beauforts of 42 Squadron, at present transferring from Leuchars in Scotland down to Coltishall in East Anglia, should join 86 Squadron at Manston. He then phoned No.11 Group and asked them to provide adequate fighter protection for the Fleet Air Arm Swordfish already stationed at Manston. It was now almost noon, and so far no attack had been made on the German ships.

The armada of ships did in fact sail past Dover without being attacked, and by this time Ciliax could not believe his luck. From the bridge of *Scharnhorst* he could almost see the look of astonishment on Ramsey's face. At any moment he expected to hear the scream of shells from the heavy Dover guns, but all he heard was the steady hum of *Scharnhorst's* engines. He realised he had been lucky thus far, and almost relieved when he saw the four Spitfires and knew the cat was out of the bag.

Back at Dover Castle, Brigadier Cecil Whitfield Raw, the Army Officer in charge of the coastal batteries, sent out the alarm to the gunners. The guns themselves were placed along the Dover area of the South Coast. One site at St Margarets Bay had a fourteen-inch naval gun with a range of 50,000 yards. A second fourteen-inch gun was sited at St Margarets Village. Two more guns were mounted on railway trucks. These were thirteen-point-five-inch guns, placed at Lydden Spout and Guston Tunnel. Three batteries of guns were located in the Dover area, consisting of six-inch guns at Fan Bay, four nine-point-two-inch guns on the South Foreland, while at Wanstone Farm a battery of fifteen-inch guns was still in the process of installation. The heavy guns, however, were of little use in this action, mainly because they were intended for use against fixed targets. The smaller guns had a higher rate of fire,

825 Squadron Badge

and were more manoeuvrable. So it fell to the nine-point-two gunners on the South Foreland to be the first to attack the German ships.

Here again fate stepped in, this time in the form of bad visibility in the Channel. The cloud base descended, covering the ships from the view of the British gunners, but this did not deter the gunners, and with the aid of their radar sets they fired thirty three rounds in the seventeen minutes the ships were in their range. Not one shell hit its target.

While the gunners were firing away, five fast MTBs were heading out of Dover Harbour under the command of Lieutenant-Commander Nigel Pumphrey. Each boat carried two torpedoes, each had a captain and a crew of eight. It was not a very formidable force to tackle the enemy force. It was almost 12.30 pm when Pumphrey made contact with the Germans, and the first time for many years so powerful an enemy had been sighted in the Channel. Pumphrey reported back to Dover over the radio that he had sighted the enemy, and the Admiralty made this their first 'official' report that the enemy was in fact in the Channel.

It was a very short encounter, however, for the German ships were sailing at thirty knots, while Pumphrey's little ships could make only twenty-eight knots flat out. The German E boats on the outer screen were capable of thirty-five knots, so could easily out sail Pumphrey's ships.

Making the best of the situation, and under heavy fire from the Germans, both from the E-boats and Galland's aircraft, the MTBs pressed home their attack. Firing their torpedoes at the capital ships, from too long a range they hoped one would find the target. Then it was a case of beating a hasty retreat.

The Officers on the bridge of *Scharnhorst* watched the torpedoes come streaking across the water at them. None found their mark as Captain Hoffmann took evading action.

On returning to Dover, Pumphrey reported to Admiral Ramsey with a heavy heart. He realised that without proper support his attack had been doomed to failure from the start, and he had been given too little warning. In a report he made to the Admiral he stated his complaints.

At Manston, the six old Swordfish were at readiness. Their

Fairey Swordfish

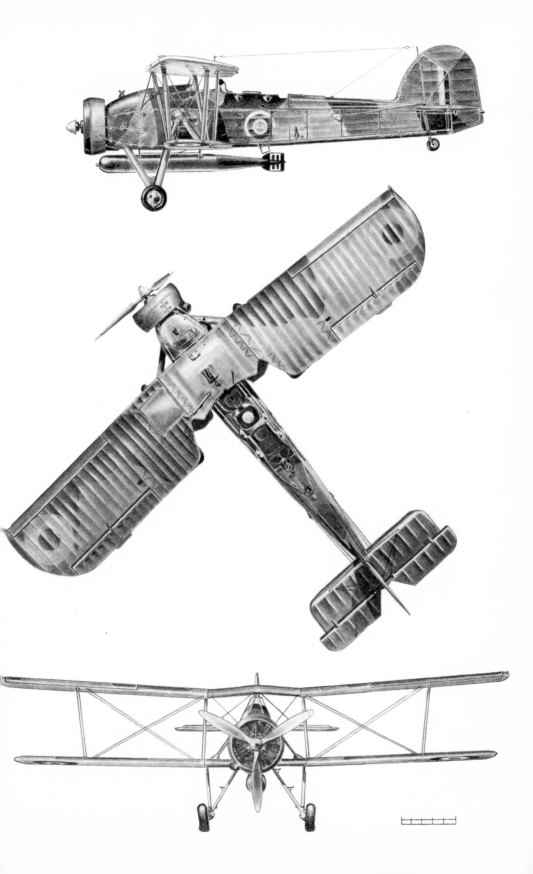

commanding officer, Lieutenant Commander Eugene Esmonde, had just received a telephone call from Dover Castle. The final decision had been left to Esmonde himself as to whether or not he should attack in daylight. When originally briefed, the operation had been envisaged as a night action. It was a difficult decision, with seventeen young lives at risk, but he knew he must go. Facing them in the crew room at Manston, looking at their eager young faces, he wondered as he told them the news how many would return. Station Commander Tom Gleave saw Esmonde as he walked across the apron to his aircraft, and wished him luck. He was amazed at the transformation in Esmonde, who hardly replied. It was as if he knew he would never return.

Five squadrons of fighters (50 aircraft) were supposed to join up with the six Swordfish over the Channel off Ramsgate, their appointed time of rendezvous 12.25 pm. As the six aircraft left Manston runway and headed out over the Channel, they circled for four minutes before sighting any fighters. Of the five squadrons promised, only *ten* Spitfires turned up. Once again fate was working for the Germans.

The Spitfires were from 72 Squadron stationed at Gravesend, a satellite airfield of Biggin Hill. Squadron Leader Brian Kingcombe was their leader. He did not know what all the 'flap' was about. He knew of operation 'Fuller', but no one had told him that he was now a part of it. He had simply been told to get to Manston as fast as he could to escort six Swordfish into battle.

There was no doubt that Esmonde was pleased to see the Spitfires, for he knew that his old aircraft were no match for the fast modern fighters that Galland's men were flying. With a torpedo attached, the maximum speed of the Swordfish was only 90 mph and she was very sluggish to handle. After circling for a few minutes longer Esmonde decided they had better not wait any longer, as it looked as though the other four squadrons of fighters were not going to arrive. Signalling to his other pilots to form up behind him in two flights, he dived down to fifty feet and headed out to sea.

The escorting Spitfires circled at two thousand feet, slightly in advance of the Swordfish. It would take them at least fifteen minutes to make contact with the Germans. Sure enough, a quarter of an hour later six of Galland's Me.109s swooped out of the clouds at the Swordfish. The Spitfires came down to assist, and soon a fierce battle developed, with more of Galland's men coming in to attack. Eventually the Spitfires were fighting for their own lives, leaving Esmonde's crews to do the best they could on their own.

Now the FW190s were in on the attack, firing their cannons at the Swordfish. Esmonde in the leading plane was crossing the protective screens of the outer E-boats and destroyers. His mind was on the target ahead of him, the *Prinz Eugen*, for he and his squadron were approaching the Germans from the rear.

Back at Biggin Hill, things were in a turmoil. It was the same at Hornchurch. Two Spitfire squadrons, 64 and 411, left Hornchurch over a quarter of an hour late. 64 squadron, arriving at Manston and finding the Swordfish already gone, headed over the Channel for Calais. They sighted nothing, however, so returned to base. 411 squadron was a Canadian squadron. They realised the situation when they arrived at Manston, and headed for the German ships, but although they reached the outer screen of flack ships and were fired upon, they did not engage the Germans.

Three other squadrons from Biggin Hill were late arriving over the ships, but in spite of this did engage the German fighters. All of them were too late to be of assistance to Esmonde, however. When they did eventually arrive on the scene, the eighteen Fleet Air Arm aircrew had nearly all perished. Only five survived, and only two of those were uninjured. The whole Swordfish attack lasted only five minutes, and by 12.50 pm there was peace again over the ships.

Just as Esmonde was pressing home his attack, three MTBs were leaving Ramsgate harbour. Again, it was only a gesture on the part of the Navy. True, they did engage and do battle with the Germans, but the outcome was a forgone conclusion and they did not sight the capital ships. The E-boats and destroyer *Freidrich Ihn* kept them too busy. The five survivors from the Swordfish were picked up by the MTBs and returned to Ramsgate.

Two hours were to pass before the German ships received another attack. This was from a spasmodic and erratic attack by the RAF, both Bombers and Coastal Command aircraft taking part. Again there was confusion, more especially among the 14 Coastal Command aircraft of 42 squadron which had transferred from Leuchars. On arrival at Coltishall, 3 of the Beauforts, which had been sent from Scotland unarmed, were supposed to be fitted with torpedoes. There were none. The nearest unit with torpedoes was 150 miles away! When torpedoes from this unit eventually did arrive at Coltishall, the German ships were safe in home waters. Two of the aircraft developed technical faults on arrival, making five aircraft unserviceable. Because of this, the other nine aircraft were held back from proceeding to Manston. Two and a half hours went by before someone asked 'Where the hell have 42 squadron got to?' When they left Coltishall, Squadron Leader Roger Frankland the Air Traffic Controller of that aerodrome, gave Squadron Leader W.H. Cliff, the officer in command of the Beauforts, instructions to join up with Hudsons of 407 squadron over Manston. Tom Cleave, at Manston, was given the estimated time of arrival of the Beauforts as 2.50 pm. When they eventually did arrive the time was 2.53 pm, only three minutes late. There were the Hudsons circling over the aerodrome, with an escorting squadron of Spitfires.

Cliff had been instructed to follow the Hudsons into an attack on shipping off the Dutch coast. Nobody thought it necessary to tell him his aircraft would be attacking German heavy warships. As soon as the Beauforts formed up behind the Hudsons, there started a game of ring-a-roses in the air, for the Hudsons broke off and formed up again behind the Beauforts. This went on for several minutes, owing to the fact that the same instructions had been given to each squadron commander, each having been told to follow the other. Tom Cleave, down below at Manston, was going mad, wondering if this was some new game devised by 16 Group Coastal Command. Eventually Squadron Leader Cliff headed his bewildered pilots out to sea, followed by the faithful Hudson crews.

By this time the weather had got worse. Heavy rain and low cloud made it impossible to see very far ahead. Finding the ships visually now would be by mere chance, and with radar little better. But the clouds were full of more than rain. Many aircraft were popping in and out of them. Bomber Command had finally

Cliff — 42 Sqn

come to life, dispatching at sporadic intervals a total of 242 aircraft consisting of nearly every type they had. The clouds were full of them and with German aircraft. It was not impossible to enter the clouds flying in formation with a Wellington unit, and emerge flying side by side with a Dornier!

The air battle over the ships had now grown to mammoth proportions, with dog-fights taking place at all levels. Again fate was taking a hand on the side of the Germans, for not only had the weather deteriorated, but darkness was soon to descend. Soon the only attack to come from the British would be made by six 20-year old destroyers, for although the RAF were trying hard to sink the ships, few of their bombs found their targets. Even fewer of the aircraft sent out saw the ships at all. This was mainly due to bad briefing of the aircrews, who for the most part were not told what their targets were. Operation 'Fuller' seemed to be so secret that the people who were taking part in it were not told they were doing so. Only a handful of people knew of operation 'Fuller', and they kept it to themselves. When the Beauforts of 217 squadron went into the action from Thorney Island, none of their aircrews knew what they were looking for, other than ships.

The Navy, in contrast, kept their units informed. Unfortunately there were too few of the latter to oppose the Germans effectively. The main attack was left to the six old destroyers under the command of Captain Mark Pizey, commander of the 21st Destroyer Flotilla. His flagship was H.M.S. *Campbell*, and his base of operation was Harwich.

When Pizey received his instructions aboard his flagship *Campbell* to intercept the Germans, he was at sea with his flotilla doing firing practice. To reach the Germans meant travelling at full speed through one of his own minefields. With him in his flotilla were *Vivacious*, *Worcester* and *Walpole*. He was accompanied by two destroyers of the 16th flotilla, *Mackay* and *Whitshed*, and six Hunt Class destroyers. Because of their slower speed, the Hunt Class destroyers did not take part in the following naval action. It was going to take Pizey all his time to catch up with the German ships, and his speed at maximum was only 28 knots.

It was nearly noon when Vice-Admiral Sir George Lyon, Commander-in-Chief Nore, made a signal to Captain Pizey aboard

Loading sea mine into Hampden's Bomb Bay

Campbell, instructing him to intercept the Germans. It would be three-and-a-half hours before they would be in action. Had they not been at sea at the time, it would have been even longer, and in fact even doubtful if they would have made contact with the Germans at all. As it was, the five little ships (*Walpole* had developed engine trouble and returned to Harwich), ploughed their way through the minefield at top speed, in line astern and without incident, for Pizey had the latest Admiralty charts which showed a clear channel his ships could use. Then at 3.30 pm the lookout shouted, 'Enemy gun flashes ahead'. This was the Germans firing at the attacking aircraft. Pizey had also been attacked by both British and German aircraft, en route. Due to the bad visibility, pilots on both sides were taking no chances. There was such a mix-up in the battle due to the weather conditions, that both British and German pilots often flew in to make an attack one after the other. By the same token, when the British ships came in to attack the Germans, many of Galland's pilots thought they were friendly ships. Ciliax at this time was aboard his destroyer, having left *Scharnhorst* after she had struck her first mine. He was not yet with his ships, so command fell on the shoulders of Captain Fein of *Gneisenau*. It was not until British naval shells started to explode near *Gneisenau* that he realised Pizey had arrived. Both *Gneisenau* and *Prinz Eugen* started to open fire on *Campbell* simultaneously. Through the rough seas, spouting with great fountains of water sent up by the German shells, *Campbell* came on, followed by *Vivacious*. On their starboard beam were *Mackay* and *Whitshed*. Last of all came *Worcester*. *Mackay* and *Whitshed* attacked first, then *Campbell* and *Vivacious*, each ship turning simultaneously to fire their torpedoes. Only *Worcester*, still heading closer to the Germans, held her fire. The Germans themselves were sailing a zig-zag course to dodge the heavy bombing of the RAF. Although the British torpedoes were running well, all missed as the German ships turned on their weaving course. Still the *Worcester* had not fired. On her bridge Lieutenant-Commander Coats was intent on getting closer to the Germans. He did not want to miss with his torpedoes. Fate was not on his side, for just as he was on countdown fire, shells from *Prinz Eugen* found their target. *Worcester*, that 'gallant

Damage to bridge on HMS 'Worcester'

little ship' as she was later called, was struck by three German shells. The damage done was tremendous, and the wonder was that she still floated, for two of the shells had caused heavy damage below her waterline. And she was on fire. Great billowing flames were coming from her bows, as her paint locker went up. Then, in spite of the damage she sustained, she fired her torpedoes. They streaked through the water, only to miss the German ships, and *Worcester* was hit by more shells. Now, with her engines stopped, drifting and ablaze, she was a sitting target for the German gunners. Captain Coats gave the order 'Prepare to abandon ship'. Unfortunately the rating who went to repeat the order was struck by a shell splinter, and those who attended him only heard '... abandon ship'. Later the Admiralty, because of this incident, struck this order out of its book because it could so easily be misinterpreted during battle. With the enemy shells still exploding round her, some of *Worcester's* crew started taking to the boats and rafts. Somehow the ship did not sink. Eventually the firing ceased as the German ships raced on up the Dutch coast. They were not concerned with a small destroyer now clearly out of action. They only wanted to get into home waters. The time now was 3.56 pm and dusk was descending on the Channel.

To the crew remaining aboard *Worcester*, the Channel seemed deserted, when out of the mist came two grey shapes heading straight for them. These were *Campbell* followed by *Vivacious*. As they approached they picked-up some of the survivors who had abandoned ship. When Pizey saw the state of the *Worcester* at close quarters, he came alongside with the intention of taking the sister ship in tow. Just as he did so, however, one of *Worcester's* engines came to life, and Captain Coats told Pizey he would make for home under his own steam. *Campbell* and *Vivacious* wished *Worcester* 'Good Luck' and turning, headed back to Harwich at 25 knots. *Worcester* could only manage seven knots, but headed for home. It was daybreak when the English coast appeared, and the little ship steamed into her berth at Harwich. She was given a royal welcome, with cheering groups lining the quayside.

The saddest element in the whole organised chaos of the British effort, was the wastage of both aircrew and ships' companies. It might have been better under the circumstances to have let the

Bow damage to HMS Worcester

Germans steam up the Channel uninterrupted. Perhaps laying a continuous carpet of mines before the ships would have been more effective than trying to use torpedoes. It is always easy to be wise after the event, but the fact remains that the only real damage done to the Germans in this encounter was by mines. Not one of the torpedoes found its mark. Neither did the bombs of Bomber Command succeed.

Later, under the instigation of the then British Prime Minister, Mr Winston Churchill, a Board of Enquiry investigated the operation. But it was a half-hearted affair, firmly shutting the door after the horse had bolted. The British public was enraged, and something had to be seen to be done to avenge the disaster. A scapegoat had to be found.

This luckless individual was Air Marshal Sir Philip Joubert, Commander-in-Chief of Coastal Command. It was his Command who had failed to detect the break-out of the German ships, thus not giving adequate warning to the other Commands. He was posted overseas, to join Mountbatten's staff in Ceylon.

The following is the Official Citation of awards given to aircrew of both the Fleet Air Arm and Royal Air Force Coastal Command for their gallant attack on the German ships during the Channel Battle.

Awards
V.C. Awarded

The King has been graciously pleased to approve the grant of the Victoria Cross, for valour and resolution in action against the enemy, to:-

The late Lt. Cdr. (A.) E. ESMONDE, DSO, RN

On the morning of Thursday, February 12th 1942, Lt. Cdr. Esmonde, in command of squadron of the Fleet Air Arm, was told that the German battle-cruisers Scharnhorst and Gneisenau and the cruiser Prinz Eugen, strongly escorted by some thirty surface craft, were entering the Straits of Dover, and that his squadron must attack before they reached the sandbanks north-east of Calais.

Lt. Cdr. Esmonde knew well that his enterprise was desperate. Soon after noon he and his squadron of six

Lt. Cdr. E. Esmonde

swordfish set course for the enemy, and after ten minutes' flight were attacked by a strong force of enemy fighters. Touch was lost with his fighter escort; and in the action which followed all his aircraft were damaged. He flew on, cool and resolute, serenely challenging hopeless odds, to encounter the deadly fire of the battle-cruisers and their escorts, which shattered the port wing of his aircraft.

Undismayed, he led his squadron on, straight through this inferno of fire, in steady flight towards their target. Almost at once he was shot down; but his squadron went on to launch a gallant attack, in which at least one torpedo is believed to have struck the German battle-cruisers, and from which not one of the six aircraft returned. His high courage and splendid resolution will live in the tradition of the Royal Navy, and remain for many generations a fine and stirring memory.

DISTINGUISHED SERVICE ORDER

His Majesty has also been graciously pleased to give orders for the following appoints to the Distinguished Service Order, and to approve the following awards:-

TO BE COMPANIONS OF THE DISTINGUISHED SERVICE ORDER

Temp. Act. Sub-Lt. (A.) B.W. ROSE, RNVR, who was pilot of one of the Swordfish aircraft sent to attack the German battle-cruisers. His aircraft was hit early in the action; but though in great pain from a wound in his back, he held on his course. Another hit burst his petrol tank, and the engine began to fail, but with unshaken resolve he flew on, and came within 2,000 yards of the enemy before he dropped his torpedo, which was last seen running well towards the target. Then he flew back across the fire of the enemy escort, and his aircraft, now on fire, came down into the sea just beyond.

Temp. Act. Sub-Lt. (A.) E.F. LEE, RNVR, who was Observer to Sub-Lt. Rose — Before the Swordfish had reached the enemy escort vessels their air gunner was killed. Sub-Lt. Lee stood up in the cockpit and directed the pilot so that he could evade the attacking enemy fighters. He went on doing this until his aircraft came down in flames. Then, although under fierce fire from the enemy, he got his wounded pilot, who was very much heavier than he, into his dinghy, and returned to the aircraft, but found it sinking. For an hour and a half he stayed in the flooded dinghy, tending and encouraging his wounded pilot, and never loosing heart, until both were rescued.

Temp. Act. Sub-Lt. (A.) C.M. KINGSMILL, RNVR, and Sub-Lt. (A.) R. McC. SAMPLES, RNVR, who were pilot and observer of a Swordfish that was badly hit early in the action by cannon shells from an enemy fighter. Both were wounded but with part of the aircraft shot away, and the engine and upper wing in flames, they flew on undaunted until they had taken aim and fired their torpedo. They then turned and tried to come down near some ships, but these opened fire, so they flew on until their engine stopped, and their aircraft came down into the sea. Soon afterwards they were picked up, still cheerful and dauntless by one of H.M. vessels.

THE CONSPICUOUS GALLANTRY MEDAL

Naval Airman 1st Cl. D.A. DUNCE, who was air gunner in the Swordfish aircraft piloted by Sub-Ltd. Kingsmill. — With his machine on fire, and the engine failing, he stayed steadfast at his guns, engaging the enemy fighters which beset his aircraft. He is believed to have shot one of them down. Throughout the action his coolness was unshaken.

MENTION IN DESPATCHES (POSTHUMOUS)

Lt. (A.) J.C. THOMPSON, RN
Sub-Lt. (A.) R.L. PARKINSON, RN
Sub-Lt. (A.) C.R. WOOD, RN
Temp. Sub-Lt. W. BEYNON, RNVR
Temp. Sub-Lt. (A,) E.H. FULLER-WRIGHT, RNVR
Temp. Act. Sub-Lt. (A.) P. BLIGH, RNVR
Ldg. Airman E. TAPPING
Temp. Ldg. Airman W.G. SMITH
Temp. Ldg. Airman H.T.A. WHEELER.

The last that was seen of this gallant band, who were astern of the leading flight, is that they were flying steadily towards the battle-cruisers, led by Lt. Thompson. Their aircraft shattered, undeterred by an inferno of fire, they carried out their orders, which were to attack the target. Not one came back. Theirs was the courage which is beyond praise.

Ldg. Airman A.L. JOHNSON, D.S.M., who as air gunner to Sub-Lt. Rose, showed the same dauntless spirit. He was killed early in the action.

Lt. W. WILLIAMS, RN, and Ldg. Airman W.J. CLINTON, who, as observer and air gunner to Lt. Cdr. Esmonde shared his fate in this gallant action, and showed the same high courage.

Royal Air Force

The King has been graciously pleased to approve the following awards in recognition of gallantry displayed in flying operations against the enemy:-

On the afternoon of the 12th February, 1942, a Squadron of Beaufort and Hudson aircraft carried out an attack on an enemy naval force, including the Scharnhorst and the Gneisenau, off the Dutch coast. In the face of harassing fire from screening destroyers, the attack was pressed home with the utmost determination, at very close range. Although it has not been possible to assess the damage inflicted, owing to the extremely poor visibility, it is believed that several hits were obtained. The operation, which demanded a high degree of skill and courage, reflects the greatest credit upon the following officers and airmen who participated:-

DISTINGUISHED SERVICE ORDER

Sqdn. Ldr. W.H. Cliff, No.42 Sqn. – Sqn. Ldr. Cliff was the leader of a squadron of Coastal Command Beaufort torpedo bombers which delivered a formation attack on one of the two larger ships. Hudsons of a Royal Canadian Air Force squadron also took part in the attacks. Three Beauforts and two Hudsons were lost.

At least two hits were believed to have been scored by

Carson – 217 Sqn

Sqn. Ldr. Cliff's squadron and crews of other Beauforts saw their torpedoes running for the target as they turned away into the mist and drizzle with flak bursting around and enemy fighters on their tails.

Because of bad weather, it was difficult to find the convoy, and only good navigation brought the aircraft to the right spot. For some, the first indication that they had arrived came from the flak bursting near them, fired from unseen ships.

DISTINGUISHED FLYING CROSS

Flt. Lt. A.G. Pett, No.42 Sqn. — Flt. Lt. Pett was the leader of a sub-formation of Beauforts taking part in the attack. He is one of the oldest members of the squadron and has a fine record of attacks against enemy supply ships.

P/O T.H. Carson, RAFVR No.217 Sqn. — P/O Carson lost contact with the rest of his formation in a rainstorm over the channel. He was unable to find the convoy, and went back to base, where he got the latest information about its position. He took off again, found the ships, and attacked. He returned safely with his aircraft, holed in one wing and near one engine.

P/O G.A. Etheridge, No.217 Sqn. — P/O Etheridge found himself faced with such a concentration of flak from the enemy convoy that he flew towards the Dutch coast to attack from that direction. Here he was picked up by shore defences, which opened fire on him. He returned to the ships, and, when going into attack, his aircraft was hit in several places. The hydraulic gear was made useless, cannon shell splinters came through the fuselage, the wireless set was put out of action, and the wireless operator had an arm broken by a fragment of shell. Etheridge made a belly landing on his airfield.

P/O T.A. Stewart, No.217 Sqn. — P/O Stewart's Beaufort was hit in twelve places during a fight with two Me.109s. A bullet went through an airscrew, and a cannon shell ploughed across the tail-plane. His rear gunner shot down one of the Me.'s, which, when last seen, was spiralling towards the sea with smoke pouring from it.

ACKNOWLEDGEMENTS

In the preparation of any work of this kind, the authors must of necessity seek the help and advice of others. It is to these people that we wish to extend our thanks.

We would like to express our grateful appreciation to the following three authors, Kenneth Poolman, not only for his encouragement and editorial help, but for the contributions he made on our behalf to the Publishers.

To Kenneth Munson, who's initial help and advice was most valuable.

Mr Mike Stroud, who we constantly harrassed, but who unflinchingly gave useful counsel during the research of the stories.

We would like to express our thanks to Hawker Siddeley Aviation Ltd., for supplying and granting us permission to use drawings of historic interest, to our knowledge hitherto unpublished, in the story 'Operation Upkeep'.

Our appreciation must also go to Mr 'Jack' Collings, who was patient, kind and encouraging at all times during this period of our lives.

To Linda Locke and Marion Mitchell, who typed out our text and corrected our many spelling mistakes.

And last but by no means least, to our wives, who had to put up with our long spells of absence from their company while we crept quietly away into some secluded spot with our pens and paper.

SELECT BIBLIOGRAPHY

OPERATION UPKEEP

Gibson, Guy, *Enemy Coast Ahead*, Michael Joseph Ltd, 1946

Brickhill, Paul, *The Dam Busters*, Evans Bros. Ltd. 1951

Robertson, Bruce, *Lancaster — The Story of a Famous Bomber*, Harleyford Publications Limited, 1964

Webster & Frankland, *The Strategic Air Offensive Against Germany 1939-1945* Volume 2 Part 4, Her Majesty's Stationery Office

OPERATION JERICHO

Livry-Level, Col. Phillippe and Remy, *The Gates Burst Open*, Arco

Embry, Air Chief Marshall Sir Basil, *Mission Completed*, Methuen & Co. Ltd.

Sharp, Martin C, and Michael J.F. Bowyer, *Mosquito*, Faber

Barker, Ralph, *Strike Hard Strike Sure*, Chatto & Windus Ltd. 1963

Bishop, Edward, *The Wooden Wonder*, Max Parrish

Ehrich, Blakee, *The French Resistance*, Chapman and Hall, 1966

Richards, Denis and Hilary St. G. Saunders, *The Royal Air Force 1939-1945*, HMSO

Reilly, Robin, *The Sixth Floor*, Leslie Frewin

OPERATION THUNDERBOLT

Galland, Adolf, *The First and the Last*, Methuen & Co.Ltd. 1955

Potter, John Deane, *Fiasco: The Break-out of the German Battleships* William Heinemann Ltd. 1970

Humble, Richard, *Hitlers High Seas Fleet*, Pan/Ballantine Illustrated History of World War II, 1972

Barker, Ralph, *Operation Cerberus — The Channel Dash*, Purnell's History of the Second World War, 1972

Flight Magazines of 1942

INDEX